THE FAITH ONCE DELIVERED

THE FAITH ONCE DELIVERED

Keynote Messages from
MOODY FOUNDER'S WEEK

By
WILLIAM CULBERTSON

MOODY PRESS :: CHICAGO

© 1972 by
THE MOODY BIBLE INSTITUTE
OF CHICAGO

Library of Congress Catalog Card Number: 72-181585

ISBN: 0-8024-2520-8

Unless otherwise noted, all scripture quotations are from the American Standard Version (Revised Version, 1901).

Printed in the United States of America

Contents

YEAR		PAGE
1953	God's Answer to Man's Need	7
1954	Beware of Pharisaism	15
1955	The Faith Once for All Delivered to the Saints	24
1956	Strength and Comfort	36
1957	The Relationship of the Doctrine of the Return of Christ to Practical Holiness	46
1958	The Lord's Counsel for the Church of Today	56
1959	When God Says No!	68
1960	Claims Christ Made for Himself	79
1961	Christian Joy	90
1962	Singing to the Lord	101
1963	Reflections on Some of the Ethical Implications of Certain Fundamentals of the Faith	109
1964	D. L. Moody's Life Text	119
1965	What the Bible Demands If We Are to Understand It	128
1966	The Foundation on Which We Stand	137
1967	The Offense of the Gospel	145
1968	The Weapons of Our Warfare	154
1969	The Sanctions of God	162
1970	Our Mainstay in the Evil Hour	174
1971	Distinctives of the Christian Faith	184

1953

God's Answer to Man's Need

WE LIVE IN A WORLD of many and varied needs. Depending on background and training, perhaps, some would list their needs in quite different order from others. Those needs that seem superlatively important to a few might seem secondary in importance to others.

God forbid that I should be calloused of heart toward any need that mankind has. I am not forgetful of the fact that there are in the world today literally millions of people who are hungry. I didn't know what hunger actually was until I went into the Near and Middle East last year. There are other material needs also which men have that surely are important.

But I believe man's basic need is not material, but spiritual. For I am firmly convinced, from what I believe to be the teaching of the Word of God, that material blessing is always contingent upon spiritual relationship.

You may debate that, and with the psalmist observe that you have seen the wicked flourishing like a green bay tree, and with Habakkuk your mind may be filled with questions about the apparent prosperity of the wicked and why a holy God permits unjust men to have material blessings. I am not unmindful of such questions. But the Lord Jesus said, "Seek ye first the kingdom of God, and his righteousness; and all these things shall be added unto you" (Mt 6:33, KJV), and the things of which He spoke were material things; not prosperity, but the necessary things.

On occasion, of course, in the providence of God, even these necessary material things may be withheld. But that fact does not contradict the utterance of our Lord that God promises to care for us, and He will. His providences at times may seem strange, inexplicable; but He does care. Those of us who know Him, looking back over our lives at the times of great blessing and the times of withholding blessing, can say with God's servant of old, "There hath not failed one word of all his good promise" (1 Ki 8:56).

I would suggest to you that there are three basic spiritual needs of men. If these needs are met, other needs fall almost into insignificance alongside the grandeur of the fact that these needs have been supplied.

The world needs *a great God*. It needs a great God to counteract the materialism and the self-sufficiency that we see all about us. We have been rocked to our very foundations by the explosion of atomic bombs, by worldwide conflagrations in the wars that have enveloped the earth in this century; but I need not tell you that stark materialism still stalks abroad in the land. Though our great scientists face oblivion because of what their minds and hands have invented, and they look with fear and trepidation to the days immediately before us, still the majority of people are unimpressed and go their careless, indifferent, gay way—sure, certain, self-sufficient. I say the world needs to know there is a God, a great God to save us from the pitfalls of the materialism and of the self-sufficiency that are abroad today.

The world needs something else; it needs *a great priest*. The world needs one who can span the chasm between a lost humanity and a holy God, a priest who will come forward to deal with the sin question, to take away the guilt of conscience, to take away the fear of death, to take away the abject terror that grips the honest soul when he faces the issues of God and eternity. Peace of mind must stem from peace of soul.

More than that, the world needs *a great shepherd*, a leader, one who can come to us in the vicissitudes of life which beset us, and steer us aright, one who can give us divine wisdom, can give us to know the unfolding of God's will for us personally and nationally and internationally.

Three times in the New Testament the adjective *great* is ascribed to our Lord and Saviour Jesus Christ:

> Looking for the blessed hope and appearing of the glory of the *great* God and our Saviour Jesus Christ. (Titus 2:13).
> Having then a *great* high priest, who hath passed through the heavens, Jesus the Son of God (Heb 4:14).

The God of peace, who brought again from the dead the *great* shepherd of the sheep . . . even our Lord Jesus (Heb 13:20).

The three scriptures place together the great God, our Saviour Jesus Christ; the great High Priest, Jesus the Son of God; the great Shepherd of the sheep, even our Lord Jesus. And thus I would suggest to you that the Bible reveals the answer to man's basic need. Our blessed Saviour, who is "God of God, Light of Light, very God of very God," is God's answer to man's dilemma. Let us look at these old truths and see how relevant they are to us in this year of our Lord 1953.

Our Lord is great. We know the word *great* used in this particular way signifies His degree, His position. He is powerful, He is mighty, He is eminent, He is illustrious, He stands forth as the important one. Our blessed Lord then is the great God.

This passage in Titus does not use this description of the Lord Jesus to set Him in contrast to anyone. He surely is not great as compared to the other Persons of the Trinity. The three Persons of the Godhead are one. There is one God, and our Lord is the great God in keeping and along with the greatness of the Father and the greatness of the Holy Spirit. He's not great as though the Father and the Holy Spirit were not great.

Neither, in my judgment, is the point here that our Lord is great in comparison to the deities of man's imagination, as though they had real existence. There are other creatures whom some have put upon thrones and whom some worship, but they are not truly God. Some may worship the devil, some may worship demons, some may worship great men, but all of these intelligences are creatures. You remember how the apostle Paul put it in 1 Corinthians 8:5-6: "Though there be that are called gods, whether in heaven or on earth; as there are gods many, and lords many; yet to us there is one God . . . and one Lord."

There are those whom men call gods, and in that sense there are many gods; but in reality there is only one God. I'm aware of the fact that the commandments read, "Thou shalt have no other gods before me," and some have suggested that this infers there are other gods. I prefer the marginal rendering of the American Standard Version: "Thou shalt have no other gods besides me."

Here the apostle Paul by the Spirit of God is bringing to our attention the greatness of our blessed Saviour as God. He is God; He's the great God. We have the reminder of the fact that He is mighty, that He is illustrious; and we can never fasten our eyes upon Him nor meditate upon Him without realizing the greatness of His person. He's God! He's God!

There are two things I would like to say about our blessed Lord as God, as He comes to meet us in our desperate need to deliver us from the pitfalls that lurk about us.

He's God, therefore He demands our worship. One of God's provisions to deliver us from the earth-born considerations that would envelope us and tie us down so that we become creatures merely of sense and time, is that we worship Him. It's a provision of God to remind us of eternity, of heaven, of things spiritual. As we sing our praises to Him—not to be heard by human ear primarily, but by Him—and as we pray to Him, we are delivered from the materialism that would envelope us.

Remember how the hosts of heaven worship Him. It was given to Isaiah to see it. Our Lord confirms this, for in the gospel of John He refers to the fact that Isaiah saw His glory. As Isaiah in the temple saw the pillars move and the doorposts quake, he beheld the seraphim saying, "Holy, holy, holy, is the LORD of hosts" (6:3, KJV). These heavenly creatures worship our Lord. In Hebrews 1 we read that our God said, "Let all the angels of God worship him." When the apocalyptic seer beheld the heavens, and there was opened to him the great throng singing praise to God in the glory, he records their words:

> Worthy art thou to take the book, and to open the seals thereof: for thou wast slain, and didst purchase unto God with thy blood men of every tribe, and tongue, and people, and nation, and madest them to be unto our God a kingdom and priests; and they reign upon the earth. . . . Worthy is the Lamb that hath been slain to receive the power, and riches, and wisdom, and might, and honor, and glory, and blessing (Rev 5:9-12).

Worship occupies the heavenly hosts; how much more should you and I—creatures of the dust that we are, ransomed by the precious blood spilled on Calvary, saved by a Lord who rose again from the dead—worship Him. And so I call upon those who name the name of the Lord Jesus to worship Him, that we may be delivered from one of the besetting sins of our generation, that of materialism and self-sufficiency.

"Then were the disciples glad when they had seen the Lord." Will you behold Him this morning? Will you see Him in all His excellency, the great God, our Saviour Jesus Christ? God deliver us from the flippancy that is so characteristic of worship today. We think that with an easygoing familiarity we can come into His presence, as though He were but one of us. Thank God He partook of flesh and blood; thank God He is our Kinsman-Redeemer. But remember as well, He's the great God, and we bow in adoration and in worship.

Oh, why is it that we have not learned this lesson? I'll tell you one reason: we lack a sense of the greatness of the deity of the Lord Jesus Christ. That's the reason that when trials come, and problems beyond our ability confront us, in terror we cry out, "Who will help us?" If we knew the greatness of our God like Joshua, or David, or Daniel, or Paul, we would go on. As we realize what a great God He is, we're delivered from worry and concern, from trusting things, and from trusting ourselves.

The second word: we have a great High Priest. His greatness as such is established in many respects. The book of Hebrews provides us a number of evidences of His superiority.

One evidence is mentioned in Hebrews 4:14. When I first saw it in the American Standard Version, it thrilled my soul and I've never lost the joy of it. "Having then a great high priest, who hath passed *through* the heavens." If you are familiar at all with the teaching of the book of Hebrews, you know that the tabernacle was a pattern of the true sanctuary. There was the holy of holies, representing the heaven of God; but as there were in the tabernacle of old a holy place and an outer court, so they are in that of which the tabernacle was the pattern. There's the atmospheric heaven that we see and know; there's the heaven where the stars and the planets are, and then the heaven of heavens, the residence of God. On the day of the ascension, our triumphant, blessed, living Lord passed through these heavens—through the outer court, through the sanctuary called holy, into the very presence of God. Hallelujah, what a High Priest! Our Lord's superiority and His claim to be this Priest are established by the fact that He is at the right hand of God today.

A priest must have at least three things: He must have a needy people for whom to minister, he must have a sacrifice to offer, and he must have a heaven to get his people to.

If I know need, surely we have need. We need a priest, a mediator, a daysman, someone to come between us and God, someone who can lay his hand upon us and lay his hand upon God and get the two of us together. It was Job who centuries ago voiced this need that he discovered in the dawn of human history. Oh, for someone "that might lay his hand upon us both," he cried (9:33).

We need a mediator, and the Word of God says that "there is one God, one mediator also between God and men, himself man, Christ Jesus" (1 Ti 2:5). He is the one who can lead us to God. So my need—evidenced by a guilty conscience, by unclean hands, by an impure heart—is met, and that's good news.

But this priest, if he is to meet the needs of men, must have a sacrifice. Thank God for the propitiation of the Lord Jesus Christ. I want to say something because I believe it in the depths of my soul: before the Lord Jesus Christ ever died for men, He died for God. For the problem of Deity was to be holy and yet pardon sinners. So that God could be just and the Justifier of him who has faith in Jesus, the Lord Jesus became our propitiation. The only revelation of God we have, the Bible, speaks of our great God as holy; one who cannot countenance sin, yet one who demands the vindication of His righteousness. There must be a sacrifice, but a sacrifice which satisfies the holiness of God, a sacrifice which cleanses away the sin of man. Basic is our need of forgiveness, and God has supplied that need, for we have a great High Priest, Jesus the Son of God.

And there must be a heaven to which our priest is taking us, and he must be able to get us there. Blessed be His name, this great High Priest never loses a soul!

The third scripture speaks of Him as the great Shepherd of the sheep, Jesus Christ our Lord. We need leadership. Ever since the day we first learned to listen to the words of the Twenty-third Psalm we've known about the shepherdhood of the Lord Jesus. And I suggest to you that the older we get the more wonderful is the revelation of our Lord as our Shepherd. As a pastor, I have stood by the bedside of aged departing saints, and invariably one of the scriptures for which they call, if they have their consciousness, is Psalm 23.

We need a leader. Oh, how desperately we need a leader, and the Bible presents the Lord Jesus as the answer to our need. We need Him in infancy and in childhood, because dangers we know nothing about lurk all around us. He's the Shepherd of little children. In those perilous years of adolescence, when choices have to be made and the sail is set for the course of life, how desperately youth needs His leadership. In the days of maturity, when the perplexities of life beset us and we know not where to turn, we need the Shepherd. In the time of life we call middle age, when fears beset us and we're not quite so sure and not quite so quick, we need Him as our Leader and Shepherd. In the rose-tinted period of old age, when the reflections of the setting sun shine upon our countenance, we still need Him. And when sickness comes, when death comes, we need the Shepherd. Let me read you a blessed verse from Revelation 7 that refers to our blessed Lord as Shepherd: "They shall hunger no more, neither thirst any more; neither shall the sun strike upon them, nor any heat: for the Lamb that is in the midst of the throne shall be their shepherd, and shall guide them unto fountains of waters of life: and God shall wipe away every tear from their eyes" (vv. 16-17).

As I view it, these are our basic needs and the Lord Jesus is the answer. Are you fearful? Is your certainty about your own ability wavering? (I hope it is.) Do you understand that you can be absolved from this materialism all about us? Remember He is a great God, and He's able—able to do exceeding abundantly above all we ask or think.

Oh, that a lost world would see the Lord Jesus Christ, for He would meet them in their desperate need. If only they would see Him as the High Priest, the one who has the answer to the sin question, who can save to the uttermost; if they would only see Him as the Shepherd who can be their Leader in an hour like this.

Well, may we also see Him that way, and may we rest in His greatness, the greatness of His deity, and the perfection of His sacrifice, and in the wonder of His care. For I am concerned that you and I, instead of fretting and worrying, instead of trying by our own prowess to force our way through, would this morning, at the beginning of this forty-seventh annual Founder's Week Conference, see the Lord Jesus, the great God, the great High Priest and the great Shepherd.

1954
Beware of Pharisaism

IN 1 PETER 4 there is a text to which our attention has often been drawn, but which is of perennial significance and of tremendous importance to any age of the church. It is this: "For the time is come that judgment must begin at the house of God" (v. 17, KJV).

When our Lord Jesus was on earth, He warned His disciples against the leaven of the Pharisees. He spoke also of the leaven of the Sadducees and of the leaven of Herodians, but He paid more attention to the leaven of the Pharisees. There is something about Pharisaism that can work in us as leaven permeates dough. The presence of even a little Pharisaism will develop gradually and relentlessly until all is leavened.

The New Testament reveals certain characteristics of Pharisaism. Let me enumerate four of them.

First, Pharisaism is the substitution of the traditions of men for the Word of God. Though there may be recognition of the truth of God's Word, somehow the Word is submerged beneath the traditions and the ceremonies which men have formulated, thereby making the Word of God null and void.

Second, Pharisaism means the maintenance of outward forms to the neglect of inward reality. So long as you appear all right to others, that is all that is necessary. So reasoned the Pharisee of our Lord's day.

Third, Pharisaism represents that decadence which is the result of the love of comfort, of position and of materialistic power; an unwillingness to forfeit privilege; a willingness to crucify truth and deify privilege.

Fourth, Pharisaism, despite the form of godliness which it maintains, lacks spiritual sensitivity to such an extent that it ultimately leads to opposition to and even crucifixion of the Lord of glory.

So dull is the Pharisee, so spiritually blind, that in his devotion to what he calls the Word of God, he opposes the very Son of God.

We as Evangelicals are not entirely free from falling into any of the pitfalls of Pharisaism, but I believe we are particularly vulnerable to the second one I mentioned, the maintenance of outward forms and the neglect of inward realities. Perhaps that is the reason the Lord Jesus said, "The leaven of the Pharisees . . . is hypocrisy" (Lk 12:1). In unsparing terms He denounced Pharisaism. Listen to His withering words of denunciation in Matthew 23:25-28:

> • Woe unto you, scribes and Pharisees, hypocrites! For ye cleanse the outside of the cup and of the platter, but within they are full of extortion and excess. Thou blind Pharisee, cleanse first the inside of the cup and of the platter, that the outside thereof may become clean also. Woe unto you, scribes and Pharisees, hypocrites! For ye are like unto whited sepulchres, which outwardly appear beautiful, but inwardly are full of dead men's bones, and of all uncleanness. Even so ye also outwardly appear righteous unto men, but inwardly ye are full of hypocrisy and iniquity.

Sham, pretense, hypocrisy—these make up the particular sin of Pharisaism. The danger is a constant one, but it seems to me that our own generation especially needs to face this sin. As we look about us and see the abundant evidence of our own spiritual powerlessness and the results of our easy believism which has never touched the root of the matter, I think it is time for judgment to begin at the house of God.

It is not what we are on the outside that counts with God; it is what we are on the inside. A fellow editor, writing in this same strain, had this to say: "Very often it is those with the very highest profession of spirituality who are guilty of these things." He had just enumerated a list of sins which tragically are often true of us who name the name of the Lord.

> The high profession is a means of covering up the lack of true spirituality, just as a tree with abnormally big leaves may hide the fact that it has borne no fruit. One of the great evangelical leaders . . . who affirmed his belief in hell in such a vivid

manner that he precipitated a controversy in theological circles, has recently admitted that he falsified his income tax returns over a ten-year period. One of the leading bishops . . . has been convicted of slandering some of his fellow churchmen, thinking thereby to enhance his own ecclesiastical prestige. . . .

For every one of us who is discovered, I wonder how many there are who are undiscovered. Tragic indeed is the fact that the Pharisaism which we scorn and which we denounce has its counterpart too frequently in the way *we* live. There is enough of Pharisaism, plus our pride, our personal prejudices, our gossiping, our distortion of the truth, our uncharitableness, our laziness, our fondness of criticizing, our covetousness, and our unforgiving spirit to make me think that 1 Peter 4:17 is in order for our day and generation. "The time is come for judgment to begin at the house of God."

It is my belief—and it is a very deep conviction—that true faith in the Lord Jesus Christ always shows itself in life; and that if a man is truly saved, he *must* live differently. Dr. C. I. Scofield, who was so mightily used of God in giving us the Scofield edition of the Bible, and who was the author of the correspondence course which the Moody Bible Institute is proud to make available, put it this way: "A faith which does not impel to action, which does not result in a changed relation to God in Christ, which does not work transformingly in the life, is not biblical faith." I agree!

I care not how many aisles you have walked down or run down; I care not how many altars of prayer you have made your way to and before which you prostrated yourself and wept copiously, so that everybody was impressed with your sincerity. All the aisles and all the weeping and all the raising of hands mean nothing if there hasn't been a transformation of life.

I want to ask the plain, ordinary, unadorned question of each one of you, as I ask it of myself: Is it profession or is it possession?

When the child of God, one who is truly saved, is willfully disobedient, God deals with him. Hebrews 12:8 has this startling assertion: "If ye are without chastening, whereof all have been made partakers, then are ye bastards, and not sons."

I'm afraid that even in our evangelical circles we've allowed that conception of God which the modernist has foisted upon the world to become our conception, that God is a grandfatherly Person who will suffer all kinds of insults and never do anything about it. I would solemnly remind you, my dear friends, that while God is a compassionate Father, He is also a faithful Father. God doesn't want any spoiled children. When you and I willfully take the reins of government of our lives into our own hands, God chastises us. If you are without chastisement, God says—this is God's Word—"Ye are bastards, and not sons."

So if you stand before me and claim to be a Christian, and can even point to a day and an hour and a place where you say you received the Lord Jesus, but you are willfully disobedient to God and God isn't chastising you for it, then, my friend, you are just not saved.

Believe me, this is solemn business, for some of you have been trafficking in forbidden pleasures and in areas proscribed by the Word of God, and you know God's hand of judgment isn't on you. You've been thinking you've been getting away with it and laughing about it inside, but the awful, stark naked tragedy is this: the day will come when it all will be unmasked and you will see, and the world will see, and angels will see, and the devil and his demons will see, that you never knew God.

This solemn line of teaching in the Word of God is amazing because it is so prolific, and because it is so frank. As I waited before God, this message was not prepared without tears, God knows! As He searched this old heart of mine, as He spoke deeply to my soul, as I faced what the Word of God has to say about the necessity of reality as an evidence that we know Him, I couldn't escape the fact that God wanted me to say this to you.

I do not know your spiritual condition and you do not know mine, but God knows the condition of both of us. I'm absolutely sure that we can sing our heads off, and we can pray our voices hoarse, and we can wear our knees out asking for revival, but we will never get revival until we face sin and do something about it.

The Lord Jesus talked about this matter, the apostle James wrote on this subject, the apostle John referred to it, and the apostle Paul dealt with this solemn theme. I'm not here to preach a sermon, but simply to look into the Word of God with you. God help us to let it speak to our souls!

In Matthew 7:21-23 we have something the Lord Jesus had to say about this matter:

> Not everyone that saith unto me, Lord, Lord, shall enter into the kingdom of heaven; but he that doeth the will of my Father who is in heaven. Many will say to me in that day, Lord, Lord, did we not prophesy by thy name, and by thy name cast out demons, and by thy name do many mighty works? And then will I profess unto them, I never knew you: depart from me, ye that work iniquity.

May I lovingly warn you, don't allow any dispensational interpretation to rob you of the terror of these words. I—who am glad to identify myself as a dispensationalist—would respectfully suggest that the principles in the Word of God have their application in whatever dispensation a man lives. I'm not going to discuss or define biblical terms, as to what the kingdom of heaven is, or what the kingdom of God is. My concern today is that you and I face the fact that here were people of whom two things could be said:

First, they knew the language—"Lord, Lord!" I know that no man can truly say that Jesus is Lord except by the Holy Ghost, but it is easy to take the word "Lord" on our lips. Oh, it is so easy! I've done it. God pity me! I have sinned, I have said "Lord" with my lips, and have gone out to do what I wanted to do instead of what He wanted me to do!

These people knew the language, and we know the language. The shibboleths of fundamentalism fall from our lips as easily as water flows from a duck's back. We've got it all down so pat and so clear, "Lord, Lord!" But these people of whom our Lord spoke were lost!

In the second place, they did things. They were able to do things that persuaded them, and undoubtedly persuaded others, that they knew God. "Did we not prophesy by thy name, and by thy name cast out demons, and by thy name do many mighty works?" Didn't we? I'm frankly afraid that our own decadent generation, because we are spiritually cowards, finds some of us looking to the more spectacular gifts of the Spirit. Our first need is not the charismatic gifts of the Spirit; it is character.

"Did we not . . . by thy name do many mighty works? And

then will I profess unto them, I never knew you." Please get this clear: the Lord would never say that, had He once known them. Whatever their profession, whatever the particular device they used to express a decision, the Lord says that it was never registered in heaven. "I never knew you."

It is not enough to have right language; it is not enough to claim to do spectacular things. What is the acid test? It is so simple, so prosaic, so commonplace that we don't want to have anything to do with it. "Not every one that saith unto me, Lord, Lord, shall enter into the kingdom of heaven; *but he that doeth the will of my Father who is in heaven."* It is not, Do men think you are doing it? It is, *Are* you doing it? In the secret place of your own heart you know whether or not you are doing the will of God.

Turn with me now to James 2:14: "What doth it profit, my brethren, if a man say he hath faith, but have not works? Can that faith save him?"

I'm sorry to have to say there are some who think the answer to that question is yes. And I wonder if a lot of us aren't saying by our lives that we think the answer is yes. I'm here to tell you the answer is "No!"

Look at the Word. Verse 17: "Even so faith, if it have not works, is dead in itself." That faith cannot save. There is nothing life-giving, nothing pulsating with life in that kind of faith. It is an empty, dead profession, a stench in the nostrils of God. It is that which God will spew out of His mouth and with which He will have nothing to do. That kind of faith is dead.

Verse 20: "Wilt thou know, O vain man, that faith apart from works is barren?" God can do only one thing with that which is barren and that is, burn it.

Verse 26: "For as the body apart from the spirit is dead, even so faith apart from works is dead." There is no controversy, there is no argument; the Word of God is unequivocal. Faith without works is dead.

If the evidence of your faith is not revealed in the transformation of your life, and in the things the Holy Ghost is doing through you, it is not saving faith. Dr. Scofield is right; if it doesn't work transformingly in the life, it is not biblical faith.

Christianity, I'm sure we all agree, is nothing if it isn't super-

Beware of Pharisaism

natural. We have a Lord who died for our sins, who rose again, who is able to save, who has made us new creatures in Himself. If you're not any different from what you used to be, or if you are worse than you used to be—and there is no chastisement— you do not have Christianity. You may have a form, you may have the language, you may have the compliments of the crowd; but the tragedy is that you do not have Christ. "The time is come for judgment to begin at the house of God."

Let's see what John has to say on the subject. "Whosoever abideth in him sinneth not: whosoever sinneth hath not seen him, neither knoweth him" (1 Jn 3:6).

I am aware of the various interpretations given to this passage, and I certainly agree that it does not teach sinless perfection. The first chapter of this very epistle declares that the one who says he has no sin is the greatest offender of all. And in chapter 2 we read that if any Christian sins, he has an Advocate with the Father. So this passage does not mean that we can't sin.

I would remind you of the tense of the verb. "Whosoever abideth in him *sinneth* not." It is my absolute conviction that no child of God who is truly saved can willfully *continue* in sin, can willfully *continue* in disobedience, without experiencing God's hand of judgment and chastisement even to the point of death (1 Co 11:30); otherwise he isn't a child of God at all.

If we can sit back and ease our own consciences; if we can mitigate the enormity of our own sin and explain away our own perfidy and be perfectly happy about it, and not have the chastening hand of God upon us, I want to say we are lost. We are lost! I don't care whether we know the language. My Lord says it isn't the language; it isn't the works you do that count; it is whether you do the will of God.

God hates sin. The Word of God says that if we abide in Him we won't go on in our willful disobedience against Him. "He that doeth sin is of the devil; for the devil sinneth from the beginning" (1 Jn 3:8). He that continueth in sin is of the devil, says John by the Holy Spirit. "Whosoever is begotten of God doeth no sin, because his seed abideth in him: and he cannot [continue in] sin, because he is begotten of God" (1 Jn 3:9). The habitual, the continual practice of sin and our condoning it—without God's chastening hand upon us—brands us as the children of the devil. No child of God lives that way. "The time is come for judgment to begin at the house of God."

Paul deals with the subject in several passages (1 Co 6:8-11; Eph 5:5-6; Gal 5:19-21). In the Galatian passage we have enumerated for us some of the works of the flesh: "Now the works of the flesh are manifest, which are these: fornication, uncleanness, lasciviousness, idolatry, sorcery, enmities, strife, jealousies, wraths, factions, divisions, parties, envyings, drunkenness, revellings, and such like."

There are three categories of sin here. First, there are the sins of lasciviousness, the sins of sensuality, those awful fleshly sins, so gross in their outbreaking as to cause a spiritually sensitive soul to shudder. Second, there are the sins of maliciousness: the bitterness of heart, the wrath, the anger, the malice that lurks in the human heart. Third, there are the sins of debauchery: drunkenness, revelings, and such like. An awful picture of sin!

After the apostle Paul by the Spirit of God has given that list, He says this—look at it carefully: "Of which I forewarn you, even as I did forewarn you, that they who practice such things shall not inherit the kingdom of God" (v. 21). There it is! They who live constantly in these things, they who make these things their habit, shall not inherit the kingdom of God.

So, my friend, I leave it to you whether you'll believe some religious teacher and some tradition of man, or whether you will believe the Word of God. As the Spirit of God begins to speak to each one of us about our relationship to these works of the flesh, let me ask you. Are you practicing any one of them? If you are, God says you shall not inherit the kingdom of God.

But true faith in the Lord Jesus revolutionizes a man. While I do not say he cannot sin, I do say that there is a principle of life infused in him by the power of the Holy Ghost so that he loves righteousness. The indwelling Lord enables him to be victor over sin and to know victory when the tempter comes in all his fury. We don't have to be beaten the way we are. We don't have to be dragged in the dust the way we are. In fact, if we practice the works of the flesh we don't know Him.

These are solemn words from the Word of God. They search

my own heart before God, And as I've read these verses, I've said to myself, "Dare you ask for revival?" No revival has ever come without facing and forsaking sin.

Are some of us here this morning sick and tired enough of our spiritual impotency to face the plague of our own souls, and in repentance and in contrition to turn to God? Are we longing enough for revival to do business with God? Some of us who are leaders need to get straight with God. "The time is come for judgment to begin at the house of God."

Let me give you a verse that God has given me. It voices the aspiration of my soul as I face these scriptures: 2 Corinthians 7:1: "Let us cleanse ourselves from all defilement of flesh and spirit, perfecting holiness in the fear of God."

Let's cleanse ourselves. Some of us have sins of sensuality—fierce, raging, burning passions that have never heard the voice of the Son of God saying, "Be muzzled!" Will you do business with God, and as a poor, lost, hopeless sinner mean business in coming to Christ?

But there are also sins of the spirit. Our arrogance, our pride, our love of being carping critics—these are evidences of the defilement of spirit. "Let us cleanse ourselves from *all* defilement of flesh and spirit."

"Oh," you say, "how can I cleanse myself?" Bless your heart, dear friend, there is only one way to cleanse ourselves and that is to go to the fountain filled with blood drawn from Immanuel's veins. Let's get back to Calvary. We need to get back there, to get our hearts broken and be cleansed. Will *you* do it? "The time is come for judgment to begin at the house of God." God help us to face the plague of our own souls.

1955

The Faith Once for All Delivered to the Saints

LAST THURSDAY was a very important day so far as Moody Bible Institute is concerned, because it marked the one hundredth anniversary of the birth of Henry Parsons Crowell, who for many years was the chairman of the Board of Trustees of the Institute. This man of God, so self-effacing, as far as the multitudes were concerned, was an outstanding leader for the Institute, one who stood nobly by Dr. James M. Gray, so that through the years the Institute has had the name of being a place that has been committed to the faith once for all delivered to the saints.

We pause at this moment to remember the life and ministry of Mr. Crowell. We thank God that He brought him to the knowledge of His Lord and Saviour Jesus Christ, that He gave him the acumen to be the businessman that he was, that He gave him the gracious leadership of the Institute with Dr. Gray for so many years. He was a man deeply committed to the great fundamentals of the faith.

It seems appropriate, therefore, not only because I have sensed the leading of the Spirit of God to the subject at hand, but also because of this anniversary occasion so recently past marking the birth of Henry Parsons Crowell, January 27, 1855, that I speak on the faith once for all delivered to the saints.

The book of Jude gives the verse where the title is found: "Beloved, while I was giving all diligence to write unto you of our common salvation, I was constrained to write unto you exhorting you to contend earnestly for the faith which was once for all delivered unto the saints" (v. 3).

I am saying nothing startling and new to a congregation like this one when I affirm that the Bible predicts that there must be an apostasy in the last days. I take time to read just a few verses out of many.

> But the Spirit saith expressly, that in later times some shall fall away from the faith, giving heed to seducing spirits and doctrines of demons, through the hypocrisy of men that speak lies, branded in their own conscience as with a hot iron (1 Ti 4:1-2).
>
> But know this, that in the last days grievous times shall come. For men shall be lovers of self, lovers of money, boastful, haughty, railers, disobedient to parents, unthankful, unholy, without natural affection, implacable slanderers, without self-control, fierce, no lovers of good, traitors, headstrong, puffed up, lovers of pleasure rather than lovers of God; holding a form of godliness, but having denied the power thereof: from these also turn away (2 Ti 3:1-5).
>
> Now we beseech you, brethren, touching the coming of our Lord Jesus Christ, and our gathering together unto him; to the end that ye be not quickly shaken from your mind, nor yet be troubled, either by spirit, or by word, or by epistle as from us, as that the day of the Lord is just at hand; let no man beguile you in any wise: for it will not be, except the falling away come first (2 Th 2:1-3).

We are aware, of course, that this word translated "the falling away" when transliterated into English is our very word *apostasy*. "Let no man beguile you in any wise: for the day of the Lord will not be except the apostasy come first."

There is no need to labor the point that unbelief stalks abroad not only in the land but in the church. The meliorists with their social gospel deny the fundamentals of the faith. The neoorthodox —the modernists who have swung back to a more conservative position—have not really adopted the fundamentals of the faith. But such tenets, for example, as the objective historic revelation of God in the Holy Scriptures and the absolute necessity of the bodily resurrection of our Lord, are denied by them. Indeed, the great doctrines of the Word of God are left to the predilection of the individual.

Apostasy stalks abroad! It is nothing for respected church leaders to deny the virgin birth, to make fun of verbal inspiration, to brand the substitutionary atonement as a medieval superstition, and to laugh out of court any personal return of our Lord—and get away with such disavowals of the faith.

There are many points of disagreement between the modernist and his unbelief, on the one side, and the fundamentalist and his belief, on the other. However, in my judgment, there is one basic area which is the source of all the difference. The center of the controversy between belief and unbelief, between fundamentalism and modernism, is whether we have the complete and final revelation of God in the Bible. If we have an objective standard verbally inspired, then every other fundamental truth must flow from it.

For example, the man who believes the Bible is in deed and in truth the Word of God believes in the virgin birth, believes in the sinless life, the atoning death, the bodily resurrection, the ascension and the return of the Lord Jesus. To such a man the deity of Christ is not in question. On the other hand, if there is no infallible and inerrant word from God, then man is on a ceaseless quest for truth. He has yet to find an authoritative objective standard of anything. The best he can do is to reach tentative conclusions on the basis of experience, or reason, or intuition. Of such an individual 2 Timothy 3:7 is very much to the point; he is ever learning and never able to come to the knowledge of the truth.

The fundamentalist believes that the Word of God is his objective standard. However limited his understanding may be, however short his experience of the truth, the fundamentalist at least has the revelation of which the Lord Jesus said, "Thy word is truth." But whatever lip service the modernist pays the Bible, it is not for him the final rule of faith and practice.

Moody Bible Institute, through the years and still today, affirms gladly and strongly that the great truths of the Word of God give us "the faith which was once for all delivered to the saints." God has spoken. We simply ask, "What does God say?" Is the faith *once for all* delivered, or is it not? Is it to the law and to the testimony, and if they speak not according to this word there is no light in them, or is it not? Will not one jot or tittle pass away until all is fulfilled, or will it? Did the Holy Spirit reveal all the truth to the disciples, or did He not? In short, did our Lord know what He was talking about, or did He not?

"Beloved, while I was giving all diligence to write unto you of our common salvation, I was constrained to write unto you exhorting you to contend earnestly for the faith which was once for all delivered unto the saints" (Jude 3). That is the Word of God.

"To the law and to the testimony: if they speak not according to this word, it is because there is no light in them" (Is 8:20, KJV). That is the Word of God.

"For verily I say unto you, Till heaven and earth pass away, one jot or one tittle shall in no wise pass away from the law, till all things be accomplished" (Mt 5:18). That is the Word of God.

"If he called them gods, unto whom the word of God came (and the scripture cannot be broken), say ye of him, whom the Father sanctified and sent into the world, Thou blasphemest; because I said, I am the Son of God?" (Jn 10:35). That is the Word of God.

"I have yet many things to say unto you, but ye cannot bear them now. Howbeit when he, the Spirit of truth, is come, he shall guide you into all the truth" (Jn 16:13). That is the Word of God.

Years ago there labored in Germany a very eminent and excellent teacher whose name was Franz Delitzsch, a German exegete of the highest water, no mean Hebraist. He died in 1890. While he was teaching at Leipzig, it is said that on one occasion he turned to his students and said, "Young gentlemen, the battle is now raging around the Old Testament. Soon it will pass into the New Testament field—it is already beginning. Finally it will press forward to the citadel of your faith—the Person of Jesus Christ. There the last struggle will occur. I shall not be here then, but some of you will. Be true to Christ. Stand up for Him. Preach Christ and Him crucified." That prediction has been fulfilled.

The great doctrines of the Word of God may be spoken of as *the faith*. That expression, "the faith," occurs many times in the New Testament.

The word *faith* is used in at least three ways in the New Testament. The most common way is to express the idea of trust; it's our faith in the Lord Jesus, our trust, that brings us into saving relation with Him. The word is used that way many times in the New Testament.

The word is also used in the sense of fidelity or trustworthiness (Gal 5:22; Ro 3:3).

The word is often used in a third way, and it is that use of the word in which I am particularly interested today. It is "the faith."

Actually the definite article is used with the word *faith* many times in the New Testament. Not always does it have the significance of setting forth a doctrinal, factual presentation of the truths of Christianity, but on occasion it does. For example, in Galatians 1:22-23: "And I was still unknown by face unto the churches of Judea which were in Christ: but they only heard say, He that once persecuted us now preacheth *the faith* of which he once made havoc; and they glorified God in me." "He . . . preacheth the faith."

So we have references to "the faith" by those who are skilled in biblical interpretation as "the system of truths revealed in the Holy Scriptures"; "the different articles of our belief"; "the teaching of the gospel"; "the faith that is believed objectively, the gospel."

What does the Word of God say is the attitude of some men toward the faith? What does it say our attitude should be? For a little while let us look at several passages of Scripture in which this expression "the faith" occurs. Let us see first of all the words used to describe *the wrong relationship to the faith*.

"O Timothy, guard that which is committed unto thee, turning away from the profane babblings and oppositions of the knowledge which is falsely so called; which some professing have *erred concerning the faith*" (1 Ti 6:20-21).

There is a parallel reference in 1 Timothy 6:10: "The love of money is a root of all kinds of evil: which some reaching after have been led astray from the faith, and have pierced themselves through with many sorrows."

We see from these passages that so far as Christian truth is concerned, so far as the objective revelation of God in the Holy Scriptures is concerned, it is possible for men to err therefrom. They can deviate, swerve, turn from the truth.

I would agree with Dr. C. I. Scofield in this connection. He suggests that what we have here is a possibility for those who are truly the children of God. A person may know the Lord, and yet because of ignorance or because of the snares of the devil may err concerning the faith. That doesn't mean he denies the faith; that doesn't mean he has apostatized, but it means that in some essential, in some part of the revelation of God, he has erred.

There is a second word which is used, and in my judgment it is a far more terrifying word: "But if any provideth not for his own, and specially his own household, *he hath denied the faith*, and is worse than an unbeliever" (1 Ti 5:8).

It is possible, of course, to deny the faith by voice or by pen. A man may repudiate the great teachings of the Word of God and thus deny the faith. He may write books which do this—believe you me there are plenty of them. You may tune in your radio and hear this man as he gives vent orally to his disbelief in the Word of God, his denial of the faith. But God isn't content to let the matter stop there. He doesn't stand by and say that to deny the faith means simply to articulate a few words in which you assert your disbelief in the virgin birth, in the impeccable life, in the atoning death, in the physical resurrection, in the actual coming again of the Lord Jesus. Make no mistake, that is denying the faith, that is apostatizing. But God goes further.

Did you catch what we read in 1 Timothy 5:8? Here is a man who so far as profession is concerned stands among the people of God. He is identified, at least outwardly, with the local church. But Paul, by the Spirit of God, says that if there is a man who doesn't provide for his own, especially his own household, he has denied the faith. It's not something he's said; it's not something he's written; it's his failure to take care of his own family physically, materially. The emphasis of the Word of God is not merely on what we say; it's on what we are and what we do. Not only is an apostate one who orally speaks his disbelief, but he is an apostate who in pious unconcern gathers his filthy, unholy garments of self-righteousness about him and fails to take care of his own family. That too is apostasy, that too is denying the faith!

There's a third word: "Even as Jannes and Jambres withstood Moses, so do these also *withstand the truth*; men corrupted in mind, reprobate concerning the faith" (2 Ti 3:8).

This passage speaks of those who have a form of godliness but who have denied the power thereof, and of them it says that they withstand the truth. They are corrupted in mind; they are reprobate concerning the faith.

It is amazing to me as I read the Word of God to find God's evaluation of the man who denies the faith. In the book of Jude you see God's description of this individual. I would remind you that this man who denies the faith, this man who has a form of godliness but who has denied the power of the gospel, may be very learned by the world's standards, he may be very moral as men count morality; yes, he may be far more personable than some real Christians; but God's description of him brands him for what he really is. This is God's Word:

> But these rail at whatsoever things they know not: and what they understand naturally, like the creatures without reason, in these things are they destroyed. Woe unto them! For they went in the way of Cain, and ran riotously in the error of Balaam for hire, and perished in the gainsaying of Korah. These are they who are hidden rocks in your love-feasts when they feast with you, shepherds that without fear feed themselves; clouds without water, carried along by winds; autumn trees without fruit, twice dead, plucked up by the roots; wild waves of the sea, foaming out their own shame; wandering stars, for whom the blackness of darkness hath been reserved for ever. These are murmurers, complainers, walking after their lusts (and their mouth speaketh great swelling words), showing respect of persons for the sake of advantage (Jude 10-13, 16).

Whatever man's estimation may be, this is what God sees them to be. So in 2 Timothy 3 there are three expressions: first, they withstand the truth, they resist it, they are set against it; second, they are corrupted in mind; and, third, they are reprobate concerning the faith. That final expression means that they are abandoned —they're lost, they're condemned. I don't know of any word that gives more pause to my soul, that causes me to tremble more than that word "abandoned." "Reprobate"—that's the word used of these men, reprobate concerning the faith. Err, deny, reprobate— these are the three words used to describe the wrong relationship to the faith, and alas, many, many fall into these three categories.

In the second place, think with me of the words used to describe *the right relationship to the faith:* "Deacons in like manner must be grave, not double-tongued, not given to much wine, not greedy of filthy lucre; holding the mystery of the faith in a pure conscience" (1 Ti 3:8-9).

I recognize that this is a word directed toward a group which had special responsibilities in the early church—the deacons. Most of our churches, following the example of Scripture, have deacons (whether they be the so-called laymen set apart for some specific ministry, or it be a term used of the ministry itself). But we do not exhaust the application of this text when we apply it to the deacons.

All of us surely should hold the faith—"holding the mystery of the faith in a pure conscience." We are to hold the faith! And I would lovingly remind you, you cannot hold the faith unless you are held by the faith. If there is anyone who is obnoxious to God, it seems to me, it's the man who says he holds the faith and whose life says that he doesn't. "Holding the mystery of the faith in a pure conscience." Get hold of that phrase—"in a pure conscience." It is not just a matter of holding the mystery of the faith, but holding it in a pure conscience. Under God our lives are to be right before Him; sin is to be dealt with and confessed and forsaken; as children of God there is to be a heart cry for holiness in us.

Look at a second word in the book of Titus. Writing to Titus, who was charged with the responsibility of ministry among the Cretans, the apostle says: "One of themselves, a prophet of their own, said, Cretans are always liars, evil beasts, idle gluttons. This testimony is true" (1:12-13).

That's an amazing declaration. I tell you there was no pulling punches, there was no beating around the bush, there was nothing mealy mouthed about this. Paul didn't say, "Titus, get a few of them off in a corner somewhere, give them a few good lectures in doctrine, and have them memorize some articles of religion." That's all right, I'm not preaching against it; that has its place. But that's not Paul's emphasis here. He says, "Rebuke them sharply, that they may be sound in the faith."

What does that mean? That they won't lie! That they won't be gluttonous! That they won't give themselves to the expression of their old man, the flesh! To be sound in the faith means to reject Jewish fables and commandments of men who turn away from the truth, but it also means the dedication of one's life to God. That's soundness in the faith.

In 1 Peter 5:8 is another word: "Your adversary the devil, as a roaring lion, walketh about, seeking whom he may devour: whom withstand stedfast in your faith, knowing that the same sufferings are accomplished in your brethren who are in the world."

Be firm, be steadfast in the faith. These words describe what our attitude should be to this glorious faith of our fathers, this faith which was once for all delivered to the saints. We are to hold it and cherish it; we are to be sound in it; we are to be steadfast in it.

In the final place, we are to strive and to contend for it: "Only let your manner of life be worthy of the gospel of Christ: that, whether I come and see you or be absent, I may hear of your state, that ye stand fast in one spirit, *with one soul striving for the faith* of the gospel; and in nothing affrighted by the adversaries: which is for them an evident token of perdition, but of your salvation, and that from God" (Phil 1:27-28).

"With one soul striving for the faith of the gospel." "I was constrained to write unto you exhorting you to contend earnestly for the faith which was once for all delivered unto the saints" (Jude 3). Strive for it, contend for it.

I am aware that there's another verse in the Word of God which says, "The Lord's servant must not strive, but be gentle towards all" (2 Ti 2:24). It may interest you to know that the verb in each of these three verses is a quite different one in the original language, and there is no contradiction.

Surely the Lord's servant is not to strive, but to be gentle toward all. God help us to be that, and not to enter a fight simply for the sake of a fight; not to go around with a chip on our shoulder waiting for somebody to push it off so we can slug him! But do not confuse gentleness with lack of conviction. Do not make the mistake of saying the Bible teaches that Christians should be spineless and like jellyfish, a sort of Mr. Milquetoast, convictionless. The Bible nowhere presents any such picture of the child of God.

It is true that contending without spiritual grace is quarreling, but it is equally true that edification without contending is indifference. The child of God is a soldier; he's to stand for the truth of God. Our weapons are not carnal, but we have the weapon of prayer in the Holy Ghost, the weapon of the knowledge of the Word of God, the weapon of a life of holiness, the weapon of a faithful witness that takes a stand courageously for God, with the shield of faith and the sword of the Spirit, with a stand for the Word of God.

Let me ask you, my friend, are you standing? Are you striving?

The Faith Once for All Delivered to the Saints

Are you contending? Do men know where you stand, or have you drifted with the crowd? We're living in a precarious day when it looks as though everybody can get along with everybody else. Well, I'm here to say that here's one man who can't get along with everybody else!

The late Dr. J. Gresham Machen, the champion of the faith that he was, addressed a great company at a Founder's Week Conference back in 1924. He spoke on the subject, "Honesty and Freedom in the Christian Ministry," and among other things he said these words that I want to read to you. Follow carefully, please, for I want these words of Dr. Machen's to speak for me, even as they spoke for Dr. James M. Gray, who quoted them in his address to the graduating class of August, 1924. So, following if you will in apostolic succession, I want to voice these words:

> Paganism has made many efforts to disrupt the Christian faith, but never a more insistent or a more insidious effort than it is making today.
>
> There are three possible attitudes which you may take in the present conflict. In the first place, you may stand for Christ. That is best. In the second place, you may stand for anti-Christian modernism. That is next best. In the third place, you may be neutral. This is perhaps worst of all.
>
> The worst sin today is to say that you agree with the Christian faith and believe in the Bible, but then make common cause with those who deny the basic facts of Christianity. Never was it more obviously true that he that is not with Christ is against Him.

I speak again for myself, and in words of my own choosing. No, I cannot hear my Lord branded as possibly the illegitimate son of a German soldier and be quiet, much less fellowship with the man who said it. No, I cannot have my heavenly Father, the Jehovah of the Old Testament, branded as a bully and remain complacent, let alone support such unbelief. No, I cannot hear men laugh at verbal inspiration, at the truth of the Lord's personal return, and work as their colleague. No, I cannot sit idly by and say it doesn't matter.

The modernist, for all his claims to teach ethics, has repudiated good morals. The modernist in the church, despite all these denials, has set himself forth as an absolute example of the very thing he decries—dishonesty, lack of integrity, untruthfulness. He himself is the master illustration that truth doesn't matter, that deception is all right, that a man's word need not be his bond. He has repudiated good morals first by his adoption of Albrecht Ritschl's principle that "it is right and proper, in order to allay the fears of the conservatives, to express the new theological opinions in the old familiar words." The day has long since passed that a man's statement that he believes in the divinity of Christ or in the atonement really means anything—until you find out what he means by those terms.

In the second place, he has rejected good morals by his repudiation of the absolute standards of the Word of God which involve the facts that sin is sin, that judgment is sure, and that hell is real.

In the third place, he has repudiated good morals by his deliberate acceptance of ordination vows which he really does not believe. Why should such a man wonder at international treachery, at national immorality, at juvenile delinquency. He himself has set the pattern and his life speaks more effectively than his lips! The evil which he has committed makes him unable to stem their terrifying course—and the cub has become the lion. Yes, I must protest when I see such unbelief, when I see that to which unbelief has led: the terrible decline in morals, the impotency of the church visible.

Under God, anew I want to pledge myself, and I ask you who believe the faith, who believe that it was once for all delivered and there's nothing to be added to it, to dedicate yourself with me, that God may help us to hold the faith in good conscience, to be sound, to be steadfast, and earnestly to contend for the faith once for all delivered unto the saints.

If you would like to do that, if at the beginning of this forty-ninth annual Founder's Week Conference you would like to indicate your devotion to the Lord Jesus, your dedication to the objective revelation of God, and your dedication of life to the blessed Son of God, I suggest that you stand with me and we sing together "Faith of Our Fathers Living Still."

The Faith Once for All Delivered to the Saints

    Faith of our fathers! living still
      In spite of dungeon, fire and sword:
    O how our hearts beat high with joy
      Whene'er we hear that glorious word!
    Faith of our fathers! holy faith!
      We will be true to thee till death!

                        Frederick W. Faber

1956
Strength and Comfort

IN CONNECTION WITH the majestic passage of Romans 8:12-30 concerning Christians—those who by faith have come into saving relationship with the Lord Jesus Christ described as the children of God, as having received the spirit of adoption, as being heirs of God, then joint-heirs with Jesus Christ—the apostle very suddenly turns to the subject of suffering. Notice the subject is introduced in verse 17 after he has said that if we are children, then we are heirs, "heirs of God, and joint-heirs with Christ; if so be that we suffer with him, that we may be also glorified with him."

Now, this transition of subject matter may be sudden, but it should not be altogether unexpected so far as the child of God is concerned. You see, the Lord Jesus has taught clearly that the world hates the child of God (Jn 17:14). The apostle John indicates that we are not to be surprised at the bitterness of the world (1 Jn 3:13). The Lord told us that that hatred, despite all our attempts to live above reproach, would result in both persecution and tribulation for the children of God (Jn 15:20; 16:33). Our blessed Lord constantly reminded His disciples of the cost of discipleship (cf. Lk 14:25-33); and Paul the apostle waxed very bold and said, "Yea, and all that would live godly in Christ Jesus shall suffer persecution" (2 Ti 3:12). So, despite the fact that we are the children of God, the heirs of God and joint-heirs with Christ, the idea of suffering should not be unexpected.

How shall we face this suffering? Shall we seek it? Shall we make ourselves obnoxious so as to guarantee it? Of course not. Suffering, you see, isn't an end in itself. Suffering has a purpose. It is inevitable for the child of God and, because of its inevitability, God wants us to have strength, His strength; and comfort, His comfort. It is my judgment that any suffering borne as from Him and endured for His glory will have His reward in the future, as well as His grace in the present. So I'd like to think about our lot as entailing suffering. What are our consolations now?

In this remarkable passage in Romans 8 the apostle presents a homily on suffering and reminds us of three great truths that I should like to share with you today. In the light of our present suffering, the apostle bids us to contemplate first of all the future glory; then he reminds us of the present intercessory ministry of the Holy Spirit, and finally He informs us of God's present sovereign control of all events, of all occurrences that impinge upon the lives of His people. These are three remarkable truths that should give us stamina, should give us encouragement, should give us comfort in these perilous days in which we live.

This message is one that God has literally put upon my heart. I frankly asked Him why at first, when it seemed as though this was the message that I should bring; but so many circumstances as well as the calm assurance of prayer have indicated that I should thus speak, that I take it there are some Christian workers who need this message especially. Perhaps in the light of the events which have occurred in recent weeks, a message of God's comfort is very much in order.

First of all, in verses 18-25 we have developed for us the idea of the future glory. And this is the invariable conjunction of ideas in the Word of God; constantly weighed against our present suffering is the future glory. Let me read a passage or two which beyond any question prove what I have just said. "Beloved, think it not strange concerning the fiery trial among you, which cometh upon you to prove you, as though a strange thing happened unto you: but insomuch as ye are partakers of Christ's sufferings, rejoice; that at the revelation of his glory also ye may rejoice with exceeding joy" (1 Pe 4:12-13). There it is—present suffering, future glory. See it again, this time in 2 Timothy 2:12, "If we endure, we shall also reign with him." Suffering and reigning are brought together. This is the invariable conjunction of ideas in the Word of God.

May I say something I've said many times, but I do not think it can be said too often, for I seem to have made very little impression upon the people of God. Please, please, when God in His wisdom allows suffering to come in your life, don't cast your eyes about to try to find someone else in worse condition than yourself and say, "At least I'm happy I'm not as bad off as that person." That is utterly unscriptural. Suppose you were the other person! God never comforts us by telling us to look around and see someone worse off than we. If we're suffering, and taking that suffering as from Him and enduring it for His glory, he always reminds us of the coming glory. That is the scriptural answer. And that's what is done here in Romans 8, as well as in these other passages.

But, you say, "Wait a minute, preacher, that's that old business of pie in the sky by and by, and we just don't want anything to do with it. That's this business of living with your head in the clouds and you don't bother very much about what's going on down here. You say, 'Comfort yourselves and bear all the difficulties that you have down here and endure your sufferings, and by and by it will all be made right.'" Modern man doesn't like that very much. Well, I'd like to observe three things.

First of all, I'm for all that will improve man's lot—spiritually, mentally, socially, materially. Let's do all we can to help men in all of these areas of living.

The second thing is that man is not quite a howling success in his venture to bring in the millennium. Despite all his pleas to do something about the here and now, frankly I don't see that too much has been done. I think we still need the future glory.

The third thing I'd like to observe is that the Word of God puts great emphasis upon the future glory. Listen to Moses, and I paraphrase Hebrews 11:26: "I account the reproach of Christ greater riches than the treasures of Egypt. I look for the recompense of reward." And it motivated his life. It took him out of Pharaoh's court into a wilderness to suffer, to be misunderstood, to be maligned, and ultimately to die on a lonely peak of Mount Nebo. He had a wonderful funeral, but he died. Why? Because there was something beyond the here and now, the recompense of reward.

Listen to John the beloved: "The world passeth away, and the lust thereof: but he that doeth the will of God abideth for ever" (1 Jn 2:17). Living for that which will pass away, or for that which will abide? Listen to Paul: "I hold not my life of any account as dear unto myself, so that I may accomplish my course, and the ministry which I received from the Lord Jesus, to testify the gospel of the grace of God" (Ac 20:24). Preaching the gospel was more important than anything else to Paul, and you know all that he endured that he might preach that gospel.

Listen to the Lord Jesus Himself. Turning to those who would be persecuted for His name's sake, He said, "Great is your reward." Where? "In heaven" (Mt 5:12). And He said to His disciples, "Lay up for yourselves treasures in heaven, where neither moth nor rust doth consume, and where thieves do not break through nor steal" (Mt 6:20).

So this matter of the future glory is of tremendous importance to the child of God. Frankly, though it is blessed to be a child of God, though it is wonderful to walk through this vale of sorrows being able to put our hand in the hand of the Lord Jesus, having His sustaining comfort and His empowering strength, that is not all. Says the apostle Paul, "I reckon that the sufferings of this present time are not worthy to be compared with the glory which shall be revealed to usward" (Ro 8:18). Don't let anyone rob you of that hope of the future glory. All of God's benedictions are not now, though what He gives us now is utterly undeserved and beggars description. But we do not exhaust the blessings of God in this life. And remember, our present sufferings are not worthy to be compared with the glory which shall be.

Even creation waits for that day. "For the creation was subjected to vanity, not of its own will, but by reason of him who subjected it, in hope that the creation itself also shall be delivered from the bondage of corruption" (v. 20); and creation is waiting for the day of the revealing of the sons of God. When God's sons shall be revealed, the demons shall tremble and the devil shall quail. Then shall the Son of God be magnified. Then as the trophies of His grace we shall be displayed to all intelligences as the product of the wisdom and the grace of God.

There's a future glory; even creation is waiting for that day, and we wait for it too. For says the apostle in verse 23, "And not only so, but ourselves also, who have the firstfruits of the Spirit, even we ourselves groan within ourselves, waiting for our adoption." We don't have all that God has done for us yet, all that God has provided is not ours in experience as yet; but, bless God, some day it will be.

Don't you like the reference here? We have now the firstfruits of the Spirit. The firstfruits are sweet and wonderful; but there's a mighty harvest yet to come, and that's in the future glory. We'll understand then that our present suffering was negligible alongside that glory.

Have you thought much about heaven recently? You say, "You must be getting old." Well, I'll admit it. But you know, I've thought about heaven for a long while. I've a sort of longing to go there. There are lots of loved ones there. The Lord Jesus is there. Yes, I like to think about the jasper, and the sapphire, and the chalcedony, and the emerald, and the sardonyx, and the sardius, and the chrysolite, and the beryl, and the topaz, and the chrysoprase, and the jacinth, and the amethyst, and the pearls. The Lord must love color; He must love things that shine. I do myself. I'd like to see all of that, wouldn't you?

But there's something I want more than that. I'd like to hear from the lips of the Lord Jesus, "Well done." I don't know how He's ever going to say that to me, because I know He's going to tell the truth. But I'm so glad that the thing the Lord is looking for is faithfulness. If He's looking for great results, I don't have much to offer Him. But I remember He says, "Well done, good and faithful servant." The future glory, the glory of heaven! "When by His grace I shall look on His face, that will be glory for me."

Now, I don't know what it is through which you're passing, but if you're God's servant and if you're walking in obedience to Him, there's some suffering along the way. You can't escape it. Remember then the future glory. Maybe you're discouraged. Maybe you're saying, "It's hardly worth it all." Maybe you're ready to give up. Listen, some day the suffering will seem as nothing, the glory will be so great. Think about that.

There's a second thing that's given us in Romans 8. To me this is one of the scintillating passages of the Word of God. I frankly say I do not understand all that's here, but, oh, what I do understand speaks deeply to my own heart and to my own soul. "The spirit himself maketh intercession for us with groanings which cannot be uttered; and he that searcheth the hearts knoweth what is the mind of the Spirit, because he maketh intercession for the saints according to the will of God" (vv. 26-27).

STRENGTH AND COMFORT

One of the most wonderful blessings that any Christian can have is the faithful intercessory ministry of a friend. I don't know too much about the occupation of the redeemed in glory. Some of my friends believe that the people in glory know all that's going on down here on earth so they can pray for us. Well, there would be some comfort for us in that. I don't know that there would be much comfort for them, except as they would understand the end of the matter. But I thank God that the Lord has given this poor preacher some wonderful praying friends who remember him day by day at the throne of grace. And I stand here to confess, and to confess gladly and joyously, that whatever of blessing there has been in my life, however God has used me, I give a great deal of credit to those praying friends, for God answers prayer. I have stood in the place of temptation. I have stood at the place where I might have wavered and gone the other way. And if I haven't, it's no credit to me; it's only credit to the Son of God, and to those who prayed and God answered their prayers. I have stood by the still form of some of my dear friends and relatives. God has taken them home and I'll confess I cried. I cried because I loved them. I cried because I lost them for a while. For some of them I cried because I was going to miss their intercession. It's wonderful to have someone who prays for you. But we have an Intercessor, the Holy Spirit, who never slumbers nor sleeps, who always presents our needs to God. Oh, the depth of His intercession! He prays with groanings which cannot be uttered.

Though you may not agree with me, I believe that somehow or other, when you feel the deepest, when your soul is brought the lowest, there's not much you can do but groan. The moment you become verbose, the moment you become garrulous, it's good evidence that it's pretty much on the surface.

When you can't say it, and the burden is too big and you're bowed down and there's nothing but a groan, thank God, He knows about that too. And when the Holy Spirit intercedes, that's the way He intercedes, with groanings that cannot be uttered. Child of God, are you in a strait place? Is the way hard right now? Are there things you don't understand and are all the strands of life twisted and knotted together? It is not only the future glory—the

Holy Spirit is interceding for you just when you need that intercession.

You know, don't you, that we have two intercessors. The Lord Jesus is our Intercessor at the right hand of God; the Holy Spirit is our Intercessor living in us. Paul says that God sent the Spirit of His Son into our hearts. Have you gotten hold of that verse in Galatians 4:6? God has sent forth the Spirit of His Son into our hearts! That's where He is, and He's interceding. God knows the mind of the Spirit, and in proportion as our prayer life is indited by the Holy Spirit, our prayers will have their answer in the will of God. It's a wonderful comfort to me to know of this ministry of the Holy Spirit because it's so true, as Romans 8:26 says, "We know not how to pray as we ought." So often I have to say, "Lord, I know not whether to ask this or that. I cast myself upon Thy faithfulness." I cast myself upon the intercessory ministry of the Lord Jesus and of the Holy Spirit, and remember the Lord's word to Peter, "Fear not, I have prayed for you." Before Peter had any understanding of what was before him, the Lord had interceded.

And so, if the way is hard, there is Someone who knows about it. There is Someone who is praying for me, and I may count upon the intensity of His intercession, because God the Father knows and understands, and the intercession is always according to the will of God. Comfort your hearts. There's a future glory for those who suffer for Christ. There's a present ministry for your strength and for your comfort, by the Holy Spirit.

But there's a third thing here. It's in the very familiar 28th verse: "We know that to them that love God all things work together for good, even to them that are called according to his purpose." The sovereignty of God! I suppose there are lots of differences of opinion when we get to a subject such as this. Bless your heart, I'm not much interested in converting you to my viewpoint. And I dare you to try to convert me to yours! But surely the Bible teaches that God is in control. First of all, the Bible makes very clear to me that God has a purpose, that God has an end in view, and that somehow or other—mysterious though it is, inscrutable though it is—God is fashioning all of life toward the end of the glory of the Lord Jesus.

I remember years ago hearing a friend of mine preach a sermon on a text that I have never been able to forget, Isaiah 14:24: "Jehovah of hosts hath sworn, saying, Surely, as I have thought, so shall it come to pass; and as I have purposed, so shall it stand." And verse 27: "Jehovah of hosts hath purposed, and who shall annul it? And his hand is stretched out, and who shall turn it back?" He is able to make all things work together for good to those that love Him, to those who are the called according to His purpose.

What does that mean? It means that we do not live in a world of blind fate. It means that our existence is not meaningless and unintelligible. While isolated facts of history may not clearly indicate sovereign purpose, we cannot judge the pattern until the work is finished. And God's work with us isn't finished until He has conformed us to the image of His Son. The great, almighty God is able so to superintend and sovereignly order events that we can stand, and as the people of God—though we don't understand everything, though our hearts sometimes are broken, though our tears flow freely—we can say with the voice of faith, "We know that all things work together for good."

We know it. Why? We know it because there are examples in the Word of God that prove it. There was Joseph. "God sent me here" (cf. Gen 45:5, 7; 50:20). Oh no, Joseph, you're wrong; it was your brethren. It was the Ishmaelites to whom you were sold. It was Potiphar who believed his lying wife. "No, no," says Joseph, "it was God." Do you believe that? My friend, that will put starch in your spine as nothing else will. God is behind you. Let's not get lost in the labyrinth of second causes. Yes, Potiphar had his part, Joseph's brethren had their part, the Ishmaelites had their part; but God was behind it all, He purposed it.

David in a time of unbelief said, "There is but a step between me and death" (1 Sa 20:3). Yet, the holy anointing oil had flowed down over his person! True, Saul was hounding him. But we see God's purpose in the end, and we understand. Think of Hezekiah, with Jerusalem surrounded by thousands upon thousands of Assyrians, saying with the psalmist, "Who will show us any good?" But if we wait long enough, we'll see the good; we'll see the faithfulness of God. Maybe it's an Esther and a Mordecai. In any case, the Word of God is replete with instance after instance, experience after experience, illustration after illustration that all things work together for good to those who love God, to those who are the called according to His purpose.

We know it in illustration and, if we're old enough, we know it from our own experience. For some of the things that were most distasteful, things that we would have run from if we had had the opportunity, are the very things that God has used to teach us lessons that have made us fruitful for Him later on. We know that.

But though we had no example in Scripture, and though all secular history were denuded of any illustration, and though we had nothing we could put our finger on from our own life as illustrative of this fact, even so we know it, because God says so! I don't say we understand how it all works, but we know because we know God. So, my friend, God would direct us to His sovereign control, His purpose, His knowledge. Thank God, though it is so often apparently true that:

> Careless seems the great Avenger; history's pages but record
> One death-grapple in the darkness 'twixt old systems and the Word;
> Truth forever on the scaffold, Wrong forever on the throne—
> Yet that scaffold sways the Future, and, behind the dim unknown,
> Standeth God within the shadow, keeping watch above His own.
>
> JAMES RUSSELL LOWELL

He's purposed it. He knows, He cares and He works.

Christina Rossetti wrote a little poem about Naaman—what God did in cleansing Naaman of his leprosy. Let me share it with you.

> Can peach renew lost bloom,
> Or violet lost perfume,
> Or sullied snow turn white as overnight?
> Man cannot compass it, yet never fear:
> The leper Naaman
> Shows what God will and can.
> God who worked there is working here;
> Wherefore let shame, not gloom, betinge thy brow.
> God who worked then *is* working now.

Did you get that, discouraged Christian worker? Despite all the machinations of men, despite all the untoward circumstances which crowd in upon you, God who worked then, is working now. And

Strength and Comfort

all things are working together for good to those that love God, to those who are the called according to His purpose. Thus would our heavenly Father, through His blessed Word, comfort us in our present trouble.

The future glory, the present ministry of the Holy Spirit, the sovereign control of God—what does this say to you? Well, it brings me up short and it says to me, "Why are you discouraged, why are you despondent?" I need that message. Will you let God speak it to your heart again today? Where is the evidence of God's working? My friend, it's on every hand. And if the way has been dreary and you're tired; and perhaps there has been some experience that would bring bitterness to your heart if you allowed it, and you're ready to say, "I give up," God is telling you there's no need to give up. Because, you see, our light affliction, which is but for a moment, worketh for us a more exceeding weight of glory. Heaven is ahead, and the Holy Spirit is praying for us, and God is working it all out. And so I say, "Thank Thee, my Father," and I stand again in His strength.

1957

The Relationship of the Doctrine of the Return of Christ to Practical Holiness

MAY I AT THE OUTSET affirm that here at Moody Bible Institute we continue our belief in the fact of the second advent, and that it is premillennial and imminent; and further, that we look for our Lord's coming for His own to precede the tribulation. However, these matters, as important as they are, are not the object of our consideration now.

There is another important consideration connected with holiness which will not be involved in our development of the subject today, namely, the completion and the perfection of God's redemptive process as it relates to the believer's soul and body. This final perfecting of believers in the image and likeness of their Lord is necessary to the honesty and the integrity of the Bible's teaching concerning holiness. Without our Lord's return, the perfection of the believer is not attained, for it is when we see Him that we shall be like Him. Without the perfection of the believer, what about the plan of God, what about the efficacy of the atonement, what about the honesty of the biblical ethic which demands perfection?

Perfection is to be realized by you and me, and that realization is fully accomplished at the return of our Lord. That is an important consideration, and shows the imperative necessity of an eschatology which involves the return of the Lord Jesus Christ.

But pass from such matters to the relationship of this doctrine to practical holiness. We, of course, are thankful to God for our perfect standing before Him in our Lord and Saviour Jesus Christ. But what is true judicially and positionally is one thing; what our practice is, what our state is, may be quite another thing. We have position. What about condition? We know Christ's headship. What about fellowship? Our concern, therefore, is the relationship of the doctrine of the return of our Lord and Saviour to practice holiness —our spiritual condition, our spiritual fellowship with God now.

As I study the Word of God it seems to me that the meaning of this subject upon practical holiness may be seen in two lines of teaching. The first line of teaching brings several scriptures before us which show the relationship of the truth of our Lord's return to specific items of behavior. In other words, the coming of our Lord is specifically associated with our conduct in particular. Four areas of behavior are definitely linked with the doctrine of the return of our Lord and Saviour Jesus Christ.

The second line of teaching is more general and shows how the doctrine of the return of our Lord affects the motivation of believers. After all, we need some sure spring of action. We need some influence, some incentive, some stimulus to right conduct. And this hope of the coming of the Lord furnishes such prompting, such inspiration, such drive.

First of all, then, we want to look at what the Scriptures have to say about the effects of the doctrine of the return of our Lord upon certain specific items of conduct. Turn in your Bible with me to Colossians 3.

Colossians 3:4 says: "When Christ, who is our life, shall be manifested, then shall ye also with him be manifested in glory." Now this verse is referring to the return of our Lord; He is to be manifested. The verse actually is part of a fuller text which has to do with our Lord's resurrection, His ascension, and His present ministry in heaven. So, in chronological sequence, the next item to come before us in such a listing of events is the return of the Lord Jesus.

Says the Scripture: "Set your mind on the things that are above, not on the things that are upon the earth. For ye died, and your life is hid with Christ in God. When Christ, who is our life, shall be manifested [He is coming again; He will appear] then shall ye also with him be manifested in glory" (vv. 2-4). And so our minds and our hearts are directed toward the truth of the coming again of the Lord Jesus.

Now what follows? "Put to death therefore your members which are upon the earth" (v. 5). "Therefore"—because these facts are true, that Christ arose, that Christ ascended, that Christ is seated in the heavens, that Christ is coming again, and that you are united with Him in each of these historic facts—His resurrection, His ascension, His being seated in the heavenlies, His return—since this is true, "put to death your members which are upon the earth."

The apostle goes on to name some of the deeds done by our members which are upon the earth. "Fornication, uncleanness, passion, evil desire, and covetousness" are all to be put away.

Thus you see the return of our Lord, along with the other doctrines to which we have alluded, has a definite bearing and a definite relationship to our moral living now. In other words, we are not to commit fornication, we are not to be characterized by uncleanness, passion, evil desire and covetousness. Why? Because the Lord is coming again.

I hardly think it is necessary for me to develop all that is involved in these things which are listed for us here. Fornication is illicit sexual intercourse. Uncleanness has to do with profligate living. Passion has to do with ungovernable desire, evil desire, the cravings of the old nature, the flesh. Covetousness, which is particularly singled out and emphasized in this listing, has to do with the greedy desire to have more. These sins are not to be characteristic of the child of God; he believes the Lord is coming again. Therefore he is to put away, to put to death, these things.

If you go on and read the following verses, anger, wrath, malice, railing, shameful speaking and lying are all specifically mentioned. Thus, here in this text we have set before us the fact that there is a relationship in God's Word between the truth of the manifestation of the Son of God in His second coming, and the moral living on the part of the child of God now.

Look at the second passage. In 1 Corinthians 4 the Word of God associates the coming of our Lord with hasty and uncharitable criticism. "With me it is a very small thing that I should be judged of you, or of man's day: yea, I judge not mine own self. For I know nothing against myself; yet am I not hereby justified: but he that judgeth me is the Lord. Wherefore judge nothing before the time, until the Lord come, who will both bring to light the hidden things of darkness, and make manifest the counsels of the hearts; and then shall each man have his praise from God" (1 Co 4:3-5, margin).

I recognize that the child of God must make certain tests. A certain amount of judgment—I trust spiritually engaged in according to the teaching of the Word of God—must characterize the faithful child of God. He must distinguish between the true and the false. He must be in a position to condemn error and sin and commend truth and righteousness. So I am not among those who deprecate all kinds of judgment. But it is entirely possible that our judgment will be formed too hastily and will be entered into quite uncharitably—and these things are wrong.

Paul is telling us here that it is well to wait until the coming of the Lord with regard to certain judgments; thus we shall be delivered from the sin of unjust and uncharitable judgment. Our Lord will bring to light the hidden things of darkness. It is well for us to avoid harsh, hasty, unduly critical and uncharitable judgment.

I suppose we all, to greater or lesser extent, have been guilty of this kind of criticism on occasion. We see something and we add two and two together and we say it makes four—there can be no other answer. Therefore, we utterly condemn the individual who has been guilty of what we have seen. We have no way of knowing his motives, but we condemn him because his motives *must* be bad.

Incidentally, have you ever noticed—I say it to our shame—how quick we are to believe the worst about someone? God help us! Some idle word of gossip and our ears are alert and our minds are feverishly active. God help us! This passage of Scripture connects the fact that the Lord is coming again with an avoidance of harsh, hasty criticism.

Look at it again. Paul says, "It is a very small thing with me that I should be judged of you." I like that, don't you? I can't say I've always been able to live that way, but I like it. We get awfully bothered about what people think of us. And if the Lord should ask us to do something that people would misunderstand, we usually have an argument with the Lord that we shouldn't do it because we like to be thought of favorably. But Paul says, "It is a very small thing that I should be judged of you, or of man's day"—man's day meaning the judgments, the norms, the standards adopted by men. "It is a small thing that I should be judged by them just because I don't fit their worldly pattern. That doesn't bother me a bit." It oughtn't bother us.

"It is a very small thing that I should be judged of you, or of man's day: yea, I judge not mine own self." Does that mean Paul never looked inward to discover whether or not he was truly obedient to God? I don't think it means that. I think it means that he didn't judge so as to commend himself in pride. Paul says, "I know nothing against myself: yet am I not hereby justified." Paul understood—and God helped us to understand—that there are secrets in the innermost recesses of our hearts that even we ourselves are not fully conscious of. Just because I know nothing against myself, I am not thereby justified. He that judgeth me is the Lord, and when the Lord comes, He's going to judge.

Now notice verse 5 says He will "bring to light the hidden things of darkness, and make manifest the counsels of the hearts." I view that statement with mingled emotions. In one sense I am glad, in another sense I am in great trepidation. I'm glad because I know that when I have done something wrong, but out of pure motives, God will understand that, and certainly some allowance will be made. I have said I would do something, I thought I could, but circumstances have come about making it impossible, and I'm embarrassed. I meant to do it; my motives were pure. God knows my motives—you don't, and I don't know yours. But this verse says that it will be brought to light. I'm glad for that, because I'm sure I've offended some of my best friends and some whom I love deeply just because they didn't know my motives; they have seen only my clumsy, faltering deeds. They could only see what happened; they didn't know what was really in my heart.

But then, in a little measure, I do know what is in my heart, and with mortal shame I have to look back on those circumstances when I did things for which men have praised me but I have had wrong motives, and they're going to be brought to light too. Is it any wonder that there are trepidation and fear?

There are two things I want to say. Thank God for the blood of the Lord Jesus. I would not want to live if I didn't have the assurance in my soul that the blood of Jesus Christ, God's Son, cleanseth us from all sin.

But a second thing I want to say stirs my soul and lifts me to the heights! "And then shall each man have his praise from God." It doesn't say, "And then shall each man be censured by God." It could have said that. However little I have to offer, my blessed heavenly Father and my dear Saviour are going to find something for which to give praise. Oh, the wonderful, wonderful grace of God!

You see, in this second passage of Scripture the coming of the Lord is related to a specific item of conduct, a definite act of behavior which has to do with hasty and uncharitable judgment.

Look at a third passage. In 2 Timothy 4:8 we read: "Henceforth there is laid up for me the crown of righteousness, which the Lord, the righteous judge, shall give to me at that day; and not to me only, but also to all them that have loved his appearing."

For what is this crown of righteousness given when the Lord comes again at that day? Paul says, "I have fought the good fight, I have finished the course, I have kept the faith: henceforth there is laid up for me the crown of righteousness" (vv. 7-8). The crown of righteousness is a reward for faithfulness in ministry. Paul fought the good fight, he finished the course, he kept the faith. That's why there is a crown of righteousness of which he could talk. It will be his when the Lord Jesus comes again.

You say, "Wait a minute, that's well and good, but don't you see that so far as the rest of us are concerned, there's another reason why this crown of righteousness is ours?" Paul does add at the end of verse 8, "and not to me only, but also to all them that have loved his appearing." So you affirm: "Paul had to fight the good fight, he had to finish the course, he had to keep the faith; but all we have to do is love His appearing!" You poor, miserable, unspiritual, carnal Christian. Do you think that's what this verse means? Do you think when some lovely emotion that I in ecstacy have about the coming of the Lord thrills my soul, that means I'm going to get the crown of righteousness? You're wrong, you're wrong! You'll get the crown of righteousness on the same basis Paul gets it, or you won't get it at all.

Invariably, in the Word of God loving the appearing of Christ is associated with faithful ministry to the one whose appearing you love. If you say you love the appearing of Christ and are indifferent to the claims of Christ and are unspiritual in your living and are worldly and careless in your life, there is no crown of righteousness waiting for you. You don't truly love His appearing. So let's define the term correctly.

Once again, do you see that the apostle is talking about the return of Christ? It is at the return of Christ that the rewards are distributed. That coming should have a relationship to how I live now.

Look at a fourth passage of Scripture in 1 Thessalonians 3:12-13: "And the Lord make you to increase and abound in love one toward another, and toward all men, even as we also do toward you; to the end he may establish your hearts unblamable in holiness before our God and Father, at the coming of our Lord Jesus with all his saints." What is the specific item of conduct singled out here for our attention and related to the coming of our Lord? Brotherly love. Here is a subject about which we all can talk, but about which we all need to learn so much more than we know.

I'm not pleading for a weak, emaciated, superficial kind of affection. I know that true love always involves faithfulness and integrity. But, even so, we have fallen far short in the matter of brotherly love, of sympathy, of concern, of care, of a willingness to go out of our way to help our brother, to help all men.

So if the hope of the return of our Lord is held by us, it should affect our personal behavior in these four areas of life: morality, judgment, service and love.

In the Word of God the doctrine of the return of our Lord Jesus Christ has a bearing not only on the particular outward manifestation of our life and conduct, but it reaches into the inner being and has to do with the motivation of our life. Let me briefly mention four areas.

The second coming of our Lord Jesus Christ in the Word of God has an appeal to our sense of urgency. Our motivation is accelerated because we know that the Lord may come. I am forced to action if I believe He's coming. I am speaking here particularly of the imminency of His coming. However the term "imminency" is defined, I find that by far the largest group of evangelical Christians whom I know, whatever their eschatological view, is looking for the return of the Lord Jesus Christ. And that's what I'm talking about here; let's not argue at this point.

What was it the Lord Jesus said? "Watch therefore: for ye know not on what day your Lord cometh." Immediately following that utterance of our Lord there is recorded this additional word: "But know this, that if the master of the house had known in what watch the thief was coming, he would have watched, and would not have suffered his house to be broken through. Therefore be ye also ready; for in an hour that ye think not the Son of man cometh" (Mt 24:42-44). Urgency! We have a task to perform. Let us be up and doing. Said our Lord, "The night cometh when no man can work." No wonder our gospel hymn sounds the refrain:

>Work, for the night is coming,
>Work through the morning hours;
>Work while the dew is sparkling,
>Work, mid springing flowers;
>Work when the day grows brighter,
>Work in the glowing sun;
>Work, for the night is coming.
>When man's work is done.
>
>ANNIE L. WALKER

I like the paraphrase of that gospel hymn which has come to us anonymously and reads like this:

>Work, then, the Day is coming!
>No time for sighing now!
>Harps for the hands once dropping,
>Wreaths for the victor's brow.
>Now morning Light is breaking,
>Soon will the Day appear;
>Night shades appal no longer,
>Jesus Christ is near.

The doctrine of the return of our Lord strikes another chord in motivation in its appeal to the sense of values. You recall how the apostle Peter develops this theme in 2 Peter 3:10-14: "But the day of the Lord will come as a thief; in the which the heavens shall pass away with a great noise, and the elements shall be dissolved with fervent heat, and the earth and the works that are therein shall be burned up. Seeing that these things are thus all to be dissolved, what manner of persons ought ye to be in all holy living and godliness, looking for and earnestly desiring the coming of the day of

God, by reason of which the heavens being on fire shall be dissolved, and the elements shall melt with fervent heat? But, according to his promise, we look for new heavens and a new earth, wherein dwelleth righteousness. Wherefore, beloved, seeing that ye look for these things, give diligence that ye may be found in peace, without spot and blameless in his sight."

The truth of the coming of the Lord Jesus Christ and the associated events connected therewith in the end times are laid hold of by Peter and, led of the Holy Ghost, he says, "What manner of persons ought ye to be in all holy living and godliness?" Because the things of time and sense are all going to pass away.

For what are you living? Said the apostle Paul, the things which are seen are temporal, but the things which are not seen are eternal. Said the Lord Jesus, "Lay up for yourselves treasures in heaven, where neither moth nor rust doth consume, and where thieves do not break through nor steal" (Mt 6:20).

The second coming of Christ urges upon us the choice of living for God as over against living for the things of time and sense. His coming—mark it well, child of God—ultimately means the dissolution of all that some people hold dear, for the heavens and the earth shall be dissolved; and this world is all that some are living for. The doctrine of the return of Christ impinges upon our motivation by reminding us of a true sense of values, so our vision does not get distorted, our perspective is not out of line, and we understand things for what they are.

Please do not interpret what I am saying as meaning that we ought to be absolutely oblivious of the things of time and sense. My plea is to live for God down here and to utilize the things of time and sense for the honor and glory of God.

There's a third area of motivation, the appeal to the sense of duty, the matter of responsibility in the light of the return of the Lord Jesus. Says Revelation 22:12, "Behold, I come quickly; and my reward is with me, to render to each man according as his work is."

We can speak so glibly about the coming of our Lord and about the judgment seat of Christ! Have you ever taken your Bible and turned to one of these passages which speaks about the judgment of believers when our Lord comes again, and allowed the Spirit of

God to burn into your soul some of the expressions involved? Let me give you one example of God's dealing with me.

In 2 Corinthians 5:10 I read: "We must all be made manifest before the judgment-seat of Christ." We *must*. There is no alternative; there is no other course. This rendering has special significance: "We must all be *made manifest.*" "All things are naked and laid opened before the eyes of him with whom we have to do" (Heb 4:13). All things are stripped and stunned in the sight of Him with whom we have to do. We must appear at the judgment seat of Christ. We must be *made manifest* there.

Here is stress upon motivation. The Lord cometh! I must give an account for the deeds done in the body. I'm responsible. So I move out of my complacency, out of my easygoing ways; I have a duty to perform.

One thing more. The coming of our Lord in the Word of God is associated with the appeal to the sense of the disciple's loyalty, of the disciple's devotion and of the disciple's love.

Said the Lord Jesus: "If I go . . . I come again . . . that where I am, there ye may be also" (Jn 14:3). The apostle Paul speaks of loving His appearing (2 Ti 4:8). My friend, if there is any holy emotion in your soul of dedication and loyalty and love to the Lord Jesus it is because He is coming again, the Bridegroom is coming! A proper understanding of what my attitude shall be toward Him who is the Lover of my soul means that I shall live for Him whom I love.

Thus the four areas of motivation affected by the doctrine of our Lord's return are urgency, a sense of values, a sense of duty, and a sense of loyalty and love. You do not truly hold the truth of the doctrine of the return of the Lord Jesus Christ until that doctrine holds you, and influences your manner of living as the Bible says it should.

1958
The Lord's Counsel for the Church of Today

> And to the angel of the church in Laodicea write: These things saith the Amen, the faithful and true witness, the beginning of the creation of God: I know thy works, that thou art neither cold nor hot: I would thou wert cold or hot. So because thou art lukewarm, and neither hot nor cold, I will spew thee out of my mouth. Because thou sayest, I am rich, and have gotten riches, and have need of nothing; and knowest not that thou art the wretched one and miserable and poor and blind and naked: I counsel thee to buy of me gold refined by fire, that thou mayest become rich; and white garments, that thou mayest clothe thyself, and that the shame of thy nakedness be not made manifest; and eyesalve to anoint thine eyes, that thou mayest see. As many as I love, I reprove and chasten: be zealous therefore, and repent. Behold, I stand at the door and knock: if any man hear my voice and open the door, I will come in to him, and will sup with him, and he with me. He that overcometh, I will give to him to sit down with me in my throne, as I also overcame, and sat down with my Father in his throne. He that hath an ear, let him hear what the Spirit saith to the churches (Rev 3:14-22).

THE CHURCH TODAY, despite its largeness and its ability to exert pressure, and its tacit acceptance by world leaders, finds itself without real authority. It is all very well for those of us who are fundamental in doctrine to blame the modernists for this situation, and that there is such blame to be attached to liberal theology is not to be denied. It is all very well for us to castigate the liberal and to censure those who will not bow to the Word of God. But sober reflection will remind us that even among us in the homeland there is no Nathan to stand in the portals of government and thunder God's condemnation of sin; there is no Elijah who elicits the threats of an angry, ungodly ruler; there is no John the Baptist who would rather lose his head than his crown; there is no Martin Luther who is the recognized leader of God's people; there is no John Knox to live and pray consternation and fear into the heart of a queen; there is no apparent Wesley, and no apparent Whitefield to wear out for God. A surfeited, cynical, yet fearful world looks at all our machinery, and all our bricks and mortar, and all our gadgets and devices, and is utterly unimpressed.

You say the world is sin-hardened; it is far from God; it is beyond reach. Let me ask the simple question, Is it? Can it be harder to reach, considering the few available to reach it, than the world in which the apostles lived? Is anything too hard for the Lord? No; the trouble is with us. And I think, yea I know, that God would have us turn from looking for others to blame and look into our own hearts to discover the real reason for the situation in which we find ourselves.

The gospel has still its ancient power. As a matter of fact, God is waiting for us to do something. You know, surely you do, that God always begins with the leaders. He's waiting for us—I'm speaking particularly to the ministers, to the missionaries, to the Christian workers in attendance upon this conference—God is waiting for us to make a move toward Him and toward His will.

I speak as a dispensational, pretribulational premillenarian. I speak as one who is familiar with the interpretation of Revelation 2 and 3 according to the above view. Why should we not turn to what the Lord counsels the Laodicean church? We believe we are living in the days of the Laodicean church. But wait a moment. Too long we've been casting our eyes around to find the evidences of what is said of the Laodicean church outside ourselves. It is about time we begin to look inside. Can we shake ourselves loose from our complacency, our unwillingness to face reality, long enough to take an objective look at our own condition?

God has been speaking scathingly to my own soul from this Laodicean epistle, and I must admit that the look God has given me into my own profession has not been a pleasant one. I wonder if you will dare to put your life alongside the description the Lord Jesus Christ makes of this church and discover whether or not certain of its faults are not to be found in you? It may make some of us realize that we've been inoculated with just enough Christianity to immunize ourselves from the real thing. But if we'll dare to look and dare to listen—and God helps us to realize our desperate condition—then thank God we can do something about it with His help.

God always goes to the heart of a matter. He does so in this little letter given by the risen, ascended Lord through John to the church. Here is no pep talk; here is no challenge, in the much-abused use of that word today; here is no touching of things on the periphery. The Lord strikes at the root of the trouble. If my study has led me to understand the basic need of those described in this epistle, I find it in three words in verse 17—*poor, blind, naked.*

Will you notice that these three characteristics, these three conditions, are those which the Lord lays hold of in verse 18. He says, "I counsel thee to buy of me gold refined by fire, that thou mayest become rich. Buy of me white garments that thou mayest clothe thyself, and that the shame of thy nakedness be not made manifest. Buy of me eyesalve to anoint thy eyes, that thou mayest see." Poor, blind, naked! "Buy of me gold; buy of me eyesalve; buy of me white garments."

I want to talk to you about this business of buying gold, buying eye salve, and buying white garments. First of all I want to talk about heavenly currency—gold refined in the fire. The Lord is not talking about the gold of this world, but the gold of the world to come. What is the currency that is used in the world to come? What will make us rich in the world to come? Let us listen to our Lord and Saviour Jesus Christ. In Matthew 5:10-12: "Blessed are they that have been persecuted for righteousness' sake: for theirs is the kingdom of heaven. Blessed are ye when men shall reproach you, and persecute you, and say all manner of evil against you falsely, for my sake. Rejoice, and be exceeding glad: for great is your reward in heaven: for so persecuted they the prophets that were before you."

Then Matthew 6:19-21: "Lay not up for yourselves treasures upon the earth, where moth and rust consume, and where thieves break through and steal: but lay up for yourselves treasures in heaven, where neither moth nor rust doth consume, and where thieves do not break through nor steal: for where thy treasure is, there will thy heart be also."

Matthew 19:27-29: "Then answered Peter and said unto him, Lo, we have left all, and followed thee; what then shall we have? And Jesus said unto them, Verily I say unto you, that ye who have followed me, in the regeneration when the Son of man shall sit on the throne of his glory, ye also shall sit upon twelve thrones, judging the twelve tribes of Israel. And every one that hath left houses, or brethren, or sisters, or father, or mother, or children, or lands, for my name's sake, shall receive a hundredfold, and shall inherit eternal life."

Luke 12:21, the end of the story about the true treasure: "So is he that layeth up treasure for himself, and is not rich toward God."

Now I am sure there are other ways of expressing it, there may be other emphases that you may think of, but frankly I believe that this world's equivalent to the gold of heaven is sacrifice on the part of the child of God. It seems to me that these verses which we have read from the Lord Jesus permit no alternative. If we are persecuted, if we suffer, we'll be rewarded. If we leave houses and loved ones and friends for Christ, we'll be rewarded.

There is a heavenly currency that our Lord speaks of here in Revelation 3 as refined in the fire—sacrifice. The basis of sacrifice is willingness to suffer, to die to self and to the world, and it all results in an utter transformation of a sense of values. When one comes to the place of discipleship and in consecration yields himself to the Lord for His will, things that once mattered no longer matter, and things that were once important are no longer important. All of life is different. "Buy of me gold refined by fire" (3:18). Sacrifice!

Where is the spirit of sacrifice among us? As I've gone about, on occasion I've seen this principle demonstrated and my heart has been humbled and my soul has been refreshed as I have noticed the utter dedication of some of the children of God; but alas and alack, I see very little of it. Every once in a while I have to stop and say, "Culbertson, what are you living for? How much is it costing you to be a disciple of the Lord?" For there is always the subtle temptation to beguile ourselves and to seek the way of ease and of comfort. We don't want to sacrifice.

Whatever this word to the Laodiceans may mean to those who are not Christians, there is this word for us, and God help us to face it. The Lord Jesus looks at you and at me and says, "You're poor! You're poor!" Oh, He doesn't say we're poor as far as this world's goods are concerned, for most of us have more than we need; but so far as the exchequer of heaven is concerned, and the coinage of the celestial city, we're abysmally poor, for there's no sacrifice in our faith. If we can take it easy, if we can retain our respectability and be well thought of by our comrades, that's all that concerns us. But real sacrifice astounds us and frightens us, and we're liable to say that the one who makes sacrifices is utterly beside himself and foolish. So little are we committed to what we say we believe!

I venture to say that there is not one fundamental, orthodox Christian hearing my voice tonight who does not acknowledge at once that we lose what we keep or spend on ourselves. With our lips we pay tribute to the dictum that we must give to gain, and that what we grasp we lose; but are we living it? Enough of this business of mouthing out platitudes! How much does it cost you? How much does it cost me?

Go into the realm of time. We pat ourselves on our backs and say, "We give time to the Lord." But alongside of the time that we give to ourselves, it's a pittance, and so often it's the leftovers we give the Lord.

And what about this matter of money? I know there are those who are giving and giving sacrificially. But the number giving that way are a paltry few alongside the number who claim to be fundamental Christians. Too long a few have been bearing the burden of the many; and the reputation that we have of giving to our local churches and to missions and to institutions like Moody Bible Institute we've earned at the expense of a few souls whom only God knows. God will reward them in the coming day—the rest of us will stand there with our hands and our hearts empty.

And what about our strength? God has to talk to me about this. I'm far from perfect, but I thank God I live close enough to Him to hear Him once in a while, and I get ashamed of myself. The subtle temptation is always to take it easy, and somehow our friends help us out. They tell us that we're working too hard. Now, there are a few—I'm not speaking against them, noble souls they are—who say when you tell them to take it easy, "Man, how can I take it easy?" The rest of us are just waiting for the word so that we have some excuse to slink down into indolence and idle our time away.

"I counsel thee to buy of me gold tried in the fire," something that is going to last beyond the things of time and space. Too long I've been applying this Laodicean epistle to the lukewarm church members whom I see on all sides, and in pride I have been saying I'm all right and it doesn't touch me, when as a matter of fact it touches me first of all.

Mark it, Christian leader; mark it, pastor. Until it touches you, it won't touch anybody to whom you minister. I haven't learned very much, but one thing I have learned, that if I minister to people, God ministers to them about the same thing He has to talk to me about. And until He has talked to me about it, it is just clanging cymbals and empty words.

"I counsel thee to buy of me gold." Oh, my friend, is the Spirit of God beginning to speak to your heart? Don't shut Him out. Let Him begin to search, let Him begin to lay hold on these cold hearts of ours and stir us from our lethargy.

Concerning this matter of heavenly currency, I'd like to tell you a story I read several years ago, but I'd like to take the privilege of telling it in the first person, even though it was not my experience.

I saw in a dream that I was in the celestial city, though when and how I was transmitted there I could not tell. I was one of the great multitude which no man could number, from all countries and peoples and times and ages.

Somehow I found myself standing next to a man who had been in heaven for two thousand years. "Who are you?" I said to him. We understood each other, for we both spoke the heavenly language. "I," said he, "was a Roman Christian. I was one who died in Nero's persecutions. They covered me with pitch and fastened me to a stake and set me on fire to light up Nero's gardens."

"How awful!" I exclaimed. "No, no," said he, "I was glad to do something for the Lord Jesus. He died on the cross for me."

The man on the other side then spoke. "I've been in heaven only a few hundred years. I came from an island in the South Seas, Erromanga. John Williams, a missionary, came and told me about the Lord Jesus and I learned to love Him. My fellow countrymen killed the missionary, and they caught and bound me. I was beaten until I fainted and they thought I was dead, but I revived. The next day they came and took off my head and cooked my body and ate it." "Oh, how terrible!" I exclaimed. "No," he answered, "I was glad to die a Christian. You see, the missionaries had told me that the Lord Jesus was scourged and crowned with thorns for me."

Then they turned to me and said, "What did you suffer for Him? Did you sell what you had and with the money send men like John Williams to tell the heathen about the Lord Jesus?" I was speechless. And while they were both looking at me I awoke. It was a dream. But I lay on my soft bed for hours thinking of the money I had wasted on my own pleasures, on my extra clothing, on my many luxuries, and I realized that I did not know what the words of the Lord Jesus meant, "If any man will come after me, let him deny himself and take up his cross and follow me."

What do you know of that? The Lord Jesus looked at the Laodicean church and said, "You are poor." I look in my heart and say, "It's so, it's so!" "Buy of me gold." You have the opportunity, and in all the strength of your new life in Christ Jesus you may stand tonight and be a disciple. Buy gold for heaven.

The second word I would bring to you: buy eye salve. It is not necessary to take a great deal of time to develop the thought, but, as a matter of fact, we are blind. I will admit at once that the Christian who is born of the Holy Spirit is not totally blind. Once I was blind, but now I see. Thank God, there is some vision, but we are limiting God and coming short of God's purpose because we have defective vision.

Let me read 2 Peter 1:9: "For he that lacketh these things is blind, seeing only what is near, having forgotten the cleansing from his old sins." That's the trouble: seeing only what is near. If there is one malady above another that plagues Christians it is this business of nearsightedness. We're living for the things of time and sense. Our eyes have not become accustomed to looking beyond the horizon into the celestial city; the world is too much with us. Unfortunately, in these days when the devil is so active, the world is more and more with us who claim to be separated Christians.

Seeing only what is near—what about that, my friends? It is so easy to be engrossed in our own concerns, in our own life, in our own family, that our hearts don't beat in sympathy and compassion and love for others. It takes a sledgehammer blow from God even to dislodge us a portion of an inch from our complacency, our self-satisfaction, our comfort and our ease.

Let me read 2 Corinthians 4:18: "We look not at the things which are seen, but at the things which are not seen: for the things which are seen are temporal; but the things which are not seen are eternal." Are you looking at eternal things tonight? If you are, it will affect the way you live. You may sing about them, you may claim them, you may testify to them; but unless you have your eyes set on eternity, you are singing and testifying and speaking a lie.

God help us to start to mean business with Him. Too long we've had the right phrase on our lips, but our hearts have been empty and cold. Our disobedience speaks more effectively of our disregard for the Lord than all our pious singing of hymns of praise which only outwardly set forth our devotion. Yes, God help us to acknowledge His deity. But the acknowledgment of His deity, if it is a true acknowledgment, will make a difference in your fealty to Him right now. Don't talk to me and don't fight about this business of the Lord being Lord when you're denying it in the way you live. It's about time we get the two things together. If our doctrine is right and held in our hearts, it will make our lives right.

"Buy of me eyesalve." Where are you going to get this eye salve? Peter tells you. You've forgotten something, you've forgotten your cleansing from your old sins. Listen, if you're nearsighted and you have no heart of compassion for a world that is lost, no concern for others, you need to get back to the cross. You need to get back to that place where the wonder of it all dawned on your soul until it overwhelmed you, and in gratitude you lisped your praise to God, and nothing that He asked was too much, no command that He uttered was too great. You need some eye salve tonight, I know you do; I need it too.

How about it, pastor? You're shut up to that little work. It's a good work, God bless you in it. But does the sun rise and set on it, and is that all there is? God help you. Is your own denomination the start and the finish? Is it? I have a right to ask this, for I am a member of a denomination; I'm an official in it. But, my friend, are we so nearsighted that we don't see the onmarch of the purposes of God in the whole church? God has left us here to see to it that by life and by lip we get the message of God to the ends of the earth.

I'll be frank with you, one of the reasons I came to Moody Bible Institute was that under God and with His blessing I felt I could have a bigger part in the march of missions to the ends of the earth by touching young people. That's the only reason I gave up the position I had in the East. I'm here because I believe God is doing something and I want to be in the march.

I want a vision, a vision that goes beyond my own kith and kin, beyond my own colleagues, a vision that embraces the world. How the Lord Jesus has broken my heart with His word in the gospel of John: "Other sheep I have, which are not of this fold: them also I *must* bring." Oh, do you catch it? Our hearts should miss a beat if this is what He's doing. Are you nearsighted tonight? Buy eye salve of Him.

One thing more. "Buy of me white garments." Now, this is not the garment of salvation, let us get that straight. You're going to buy these garments. In Revelation 19 there is an important word about garments: "The marriage of the Lamb is come, and his wife hath made herself ready" (v. 7). Now look at verse 8: "And it was given unto her that she should array herself in fine linen, bright and pure: for the fine linen is the righteous acts of the saints." Many of you have thought that John by the Holy Ghost was talking about the imputed righteousness of Christ. No, the American Standard Version is absolutely correct; it's another Greek word. It's the righteous acts of the saints, and they are the garments you buy—white garments.

Recently in teaching from the book of Hebrews God searched

my own heart very deeply. In Hebrews 1:9 we read: "Thou [that is, the Lord Jesus] hast loved righteousness, and hated iniquity; therefore God, thy God, hath anointed thee with the oil of gladness above thy fellows." Perhaps it will surprise you that the word which gripped my soul and reduced me to dust and ashes before God was the word "fellows." I think the reason I hadn't caught it before was because the word "fellows" in my mind had another connotation. I'm going to change that word, and I have justification for the change. Let me put it this way and I believe God may speak to you about it the way He spoke to me: "Therefore God, thy God, hath anointed thee with the oil of gladness above thy companions."

Do you know that the Lord Jesus has companions? Moses had a Joshua, David had a Hushai, Rehoboam had the young men who were round about him; a king had companions, those who were close to him. The Lord Jesus is anointed with the oil of gladness above His companions. Who are these companions? Turn back to Revelation 3:4-5: "But thou hast a few names in Sardis that did not defile their garments: and they shall walk with me in white; for they are worthy. He that overcometh shall thus be arrayed in white garments; and I will in no wise blot his name out of the book of life, and I will confess his name before my Father, and before his angels."

> When He shall come resplendent in His glory,
>   To take His own from out this vale of night,
> O may I know the joy of His appearing,
>   Only at morn to walk with Him in white.
>
> When I shall stand within the court of heaven,
>   Where white-robed pilgrims pass before my sight;
> Earth's martyred saints and blood-washed overcomers,
>   These then are they who walk with Him in white.
>
> When He shall call from earth's remotest corners
>   All who have stood triumphant in His might;
> O to be worthy then to stand beside them,
> And in that morn to walk with Him in white.*
>
>   ALMEDA J. PEARCE

*Used by kind permission of the author, Mrs. Pearce.

His companions! "Buy of me white garments."

What is this talking about? If the gold speaks of the currency of heaven, and if the eye salve speaks of vision concerning things eternal, then the white garments speak to us of character, namely, of what we are. Oh, our lack of character, our secret sins! There cannot be a gathering of Christians as large as this without some leaders, respected leaders, who are guilty of secret sins.

It has been a sad privilege in some respects to have the place of leadership God has given me. But I've learned some things. Oh, how the Spirit of God has been grieved and how revival has been kept back because Christian leaders love their sins more than they love the Saviour.

Is God talking to you about it? What about this business of buying white garments, the righteous acts of the saints? And these respectable sins of complacency, of dependency on devices, of the primacy of the secondary, the substitution of vehemency in defense of the faith for vitality in living the faith, superficiality—we're all right as long as we speak the language. God help us! Then there are the fleshly sins in thought, life and action. And the sins of the spirit—bitterness, malice, envy, jealousy, pride, covetousness. God help us! "I counsel thee to buy of me white garments to cover thy nakedness."

What is the word God gives? You will find it in the same epistle, Revelation 3:19: "Repent," a word that we've forgotten, a word that we don't know much about, we don't know how to do it. But if we let God speak deeply enough to our souls, so that we see the heinousness of our sins and the emptiness of our profession, we'll be bowed down before Him and we'll be repenting even though we don't know the mechanics. God help us to get there.

Brother preacher and sister Christian worker, God is waiting for us. I'm not speaking absolutely against gadgets and devices and ideas and plans and promotion. They're all right in their places, but they are no substitute for sacrifice, for character and for vision. Spirituality and discipline and discipleship and consecration and obedience are the need of this hour. We must get back to preaching the Word of God and to wrestling in prayer and to giving the artless, utterly honest witness of the Lord that is done in a forthright testimony for Him. We need to get back to first things.

Repent! And isn't it wonderful, "Behold, I stand at the door and knock." He is knocking tonight, and if you will open He will come in and He will sup with you as well as you will sup with Him.

I've tried to talk to you tonight about something that God has been talking to me about, the Lord's counsel for us of the church of the present day. Will you let Him talk to you?

1959

When God Says No!

THIS EVENING I'd like to speak to you on a very solemn subject, a subject about which God has spoken deeply to my own soul and which I believe that I am constrained to share with you.

I want to talk to you about the time God says *no*, the time when God, arising in judgment, says *no* to men. I think I can best introduce the subject by referring to the fact that the Bible is never afraid of apparent contradictions. Of course I firmly believe that there are no real contradictions in the Word of God, but I freely admit there are statements which seem to oppose one another.

For example, in the Word of God there is a sequence of teaching concerning the matter of fear, and the deliverance of the child of God from fear. Such verses as these come to mind: "God gave us not a spirit of fearfulness" (2 Ti 1:7). "There is no fear in love" (1 Jn 4:18). "Ye received not the spirit of bondage again unto fear" (Ro 8:15). These texts, of course, could be multiplied.

But over against this particular teaching in the Word of God there are other texts, and in the same Word of God we read that God's mercy is on them that fear Him (Lk 1:50). The apostolic teaching is that we are to render to all their dues, fear to whom fear (Ro 13:7), and in Hebrews 12:28 the word is given that we may offer service to God with reverence and godly fear. First Peter 2:17 bluntly puts the matter, "Fear God."

We are, therefore, to have reverence and godly fear for God and for His commands, and *that* fear will deliver us from every other fear. The child of God is delivered from torment, from terror, from dread, because he has turned to God in reverential trust.

I have cited these latter scriptures that I may strike a telling blow at a very widespread misconception of the grace of God.

The modernist has for a long time pictured God as a kindly grandfather, too merciful to punish anybody. But it seems to me that that false idea has crept into orthodox circles to the extent that we think God's grace excludes the possibility of His chastening us, of His disciplining us, that we are not to fear God anymore. It is as though the grace of God precludes the government of God in our lives. But I am here to tell you that especially a Christian cannot willfully disobey God and get off scot-free.

May I remind you that disobedience to God is always a tragic thing; that light rejected deepens darkness; that this is what the Bible speaks of in Romans 11:22: the severity of God. The Lord is no weak, effeminate God. He is sovereign, He is omnipotent, He is righteous. He must punish sin; His Word cannot be broken. And the most terrifying circumstance of life is to be in the place where God says *no* to us.

I should like to illustrate this principle by looking at three areas in which God says *no* to men.

I would remind you that God can and does say *no* to rulers and to nations. They may have their plans, they may have their aspirations, they may feel secure in their plottings; but there comes a time in the affairs of men when God says *no* to the aspirations and plans and plottings of rulers.

The illustrations of this principle are to be seen on many pages of the Word of God, but I do not know of any clearer reference than the one in Daniel 4. Here our God is revealed to us as the God of sovereignty and power. Daniel spoke to King Nebuchadnezzar, an absolute tyrant, a man who would not brook opposition, a man who considered himself absolute in the realm of rule, a world monarch, and said that God would judge him. Daniel declared that the king would go out into the fields, to be wet with the dew of heaven, to eat grass as an ox, and that he would be there a certain time. Verse 25 specifies that time, "till thou know that the Most High ruleth in the kingdom of men, and giveth it to whomsoever he will."

In other words, Nebuchadnezzar, you are to learn the supremacy of God, that you are subservient to the plan and purposes of the Almighty. In your pride you have taken the position of ruler and assumed a place which is not rightfully yours as being utterly supreme. God is saying *no* to that idea and to that conception and to that conviction of your heart.

Because Daniel was a preacher of righteousness, before he concluded his message of interpretation to Nebuchadnezzar, it is recorded, he said, "Wherefore, O king, let my counsel be acceptable unto thee, and break off thy sins by righteousness, and thine iniquities by showing mercy to the poor; if there may be a lengthening of thy tranquillity" (v. 27). Nebuchadnezzar, you think that the disposition of events and that the judgments connected with your rule are all in your hands, but, Nebuchadnezzar, I remind you there is a God most high, and right now He is saying *no* to all your plans and all the pride of your kingdom. You are going to go out as a fool into the fields to live like an animal. There is only one way to stop it—break off your sins by righteousness.

But Nebuchadnezzar, as you know, did not do so, and therefore the judgments of God fell upon him. I read in verses 30 and 31: "The king spake and said, Is not this great Babylon, which I have built for the royal dwelling-place, by the might of my power and for the glory of my majesty? While the word was in the king's mouth, there fell a voice from heaven, saying, O king Nebuchadnezzar, to thee it is spoken: The kingdom is departed from thee." God said *no* to the aspirations of rulership of this Oriental despot of old.

God is the God of the nations. In Paul's speech to the Athenians, recorded in Acts 17, he makes clear that the Lord places the nations, He sets their boundaries, He determines the seasons of their prosperity and of their judgment. He is a God of power; no weak, effeminate, trifling God is He. He is a God who says *no* to rulers.

Most of us have lived long enough to know something of the tyrants who have arisen in this twentieth century, and we also know they did not have the final say. To some of us it seemed as though they had gone beyond the place of endurance; but I remind you that God ultimately speaks in judgment, and the pride of the ruler is brought low and his kingdom is brought to an end. Will you get this conception of God tonight? It ought to do something for you. He is the God who sets up and puts down. He is the God of authority in the realm of political life.

May I remind you of another quite different area of life in which the Word of God tells us the Lord will say *no* to a man. I turn to a passage of Scripture which somehow brings great concern and strikes fear in my soul; not because I'm afraid of its being fulfilled in my own life, I am not, but because it unveils something of the terrible impending doom and judgment of God which hangs over certain individuals. In Hebrews 6 there is a word concerning individuals who have been once enlightened, and have tasted the heavenly gift, and were made partakers of the Holy Spirit, and have tasted the good Word of God, and the powers of the age to come.

I don't presume it is necessary for me to enter into a matter of interpretation here; a group attending Founder's Week Conference certainly has long since understood the position which in general, at least, is held by Moody Bible Institute with regard to this passage. The scripture passage in this context that I want to stress, however, is verse 6 where it speaks of those of whom it could be said they were once enlightened and had tasted the heavenly gift and were made partakers of the Holy Spirit and had tasted the good Word of God and the powers of the age to come, that if they fall away it is impossible to renew them again unto repentance. Here are individuals who merit the judgment of God to the place where God says *no* to them; it is impossible to renew them unto repentance. It is apparent that the writer is not speaking about backsliders. It is possible for them to come back, and you and I have seen backsliders renewed unto repentance. It seems to me that this passage of Scripture is best understood in the light of the teaching of this epistle to refer to apostates.

It is a dangerous thing indeed to turn one's back on light, even if that light be feeble, even if that light be little. For there comes a place—and I do not pretend to know where to draw the line—when God says that it is impossible to renew the man who has fallen away. You may say what you want about that passage, that the impossibility rests in the lack of desire on the part of the person to be renewed unto repentance, and I shall acquiesce to your assertion. But I shall add this: that God Himself is the one who says it is impossible. God says a final *no*. This is no weak, effeminate God. This is a God of authority, a God of power, and, my friend, you'll trifle with Him at the risk of your own soul.

I move to a third area. Perhaps you are saying, "God says *no* to rulers, God says *no* to apostates; that is all right, that leaves me out of it." Wait a moment. May I remind you that God can and will say *no* to His children, so far as advance in His will is concerned. Listen, child of God! For you to persist in saying *no* to God may result in God's confirming your decision. There is one story in the Bible that the New Testament lays hold on to remind us of the seriousness of a child of God saying *no* to Him. It is the story of the children of Israel which has its focal point in Kadesh-barnea.

The children of Israel had been gloriously delivered from Egypt by the power of God. Pharaoh's army was drowned and the children of Israel were safe on the eastern shores of the Red Sea. They began their journey and God took them in a roundabout way. The story of their journey was one of almost constant complaining and murmuring. You'll remember they came to Marah where they found water, but it was bitter. I cannot judge them too severely. They undoubtedly were thirsty, and when they found the water was brackish and bitter, they complained. But God made it pure and sweet for them by a tree cast into the water by Moses at God's command. They went on to Rephidim and once again the water problem plagued them, and again they murmured and complained. At the instigation and leading of God, Moses struck the rock, and water gushed forth to provide the thirsty multitudes with water to quench their thirst.

Then they went to Sinai, and when Moses was on the top of Mount Sinai in fellowship with God, they said to Aaron, "Make us gods like we knew in Egypt." When he did, God's judgment fell upon them. After the law was given and they started on their way to the Holy Land, we read that they went three days' march to the north and came to a place which ultimately they called Taberah. Because once again they murmured against God, the fire of God came upon them and devoured the uttermost part of the camp.

In the same chapter that tells that story, we have the record of their lust for meat. God said, "Yes, I'll supply you with meat, not just for a day, not just for a week, but a month; and I'll give you so much that the food will come out of your nostrils and be loathsome to you." So when the quails came and they ate of them, the plague of God smote the people.

When God Says No!

A little later, after they had gone on to Kadesh-barnea, they sent out the spies. You will recall when they returned, the report of the twelve was unanimous. They all agreed that it was a wonderful land, a land that flowed with milk and honey. It was a unanimous report that there were giants in the land and fortified and walled cities. But there was a division with regard to whether Israel should go up. You remember the multitude accepted the majority report and said it was not for them; they would not go up. They refused Caleb and Joshua, they refused Moses, and God indicated that judgment would come upon them.

When Moses told the people of the judgment of God which was to come, it is recorded that they mourned greatly. "And they rose up early in the morning, and gat them up to the top of the mountain, saying, Lo, we are here, and will go up unto the place which Jehovah hath promised: for we have sinned. And Moses said, Wherefore now do ye transgress the commandment of Jehovah, seeing it shall not prosper? Go not up, for Jehovah is not among you; that ye be not smitten down before your enemies" (Num 14:40-42).

You remember that despite the warning of Moses, they went up and the Amalekites came down upon them and smote them. Here was a generation that made a fateful decision, that said a *no* to God that was the climax of a series of *noes* which they had uttered to God, and God said, "All right, as you have chosen, so it will be, you will not go up." Then suddenly they are smitten, their consciences are leveled to the ground, and in consternation they come to Moses and say, "Look, we want to reverse our decision, we admit our sin, and we want to go up." And God says *no!*

This story is repeated for us in the New Testament on two occasions and I believe with two different applications. Let us look at one in 1 Corinthians 10:1-6:

> For I would not, brethren, have you ignorant, that our fathers were all under the cloud, and all passed through the sea; and were all baptized unto Moses in the cloud and in the sea; and did all eat the same spiritual food; and did all drink the same spiritual drink: for they drank of a spiritual rock that followed them: and the rock was Christ. Howbeit with most of them God was not well pleased: for they were overthrown in the wilderness. Now these things were our examples. . . .

Do you get that? This thing that happened to Israel was an example to us, who are the people of God. That story back in the Old Testament is not only historically true, but it is also prophetically real so far as we are concerned, for there is the fearful possibility of that story being enacted all over again.

> These things were our examples, to the intent we should not lust after evil things, as they also lusted. Neither be ye idolaters, as were some of them; as it is written, The people sat down to eat and drink, and rose up to play. Neither let us commit fornication, as some of them committed, and fell in one day three and twenty thousand. Neither let us make trial of the Lord, as some of them made trial, and perished by the serpents. Neither murmur ye, as some of them murmured, and perished by the destroyer. Now these things happened unto them by way of example; and they were written for our admonition, upon whom the ends of the ages are come (vv. 6-11).

I hear twentieth-century Christians, orthodox Christians, saying, "So what! That doesn't have anything to do with us. It may have concerned the Corinthian Christians in the first century, but it doesn't concern us." All right, look at verse 12: "Wherefore let him that thinketh he standeth take heed lest he fall." My proposition is this, that you and I—following the evil example of Israel of old—can bring ourselves into the place where God will say *no* to us. I have seen this thing and I'm afraid of it. I have been a pastor long enough and I have been associated with schools long enough to have seen this fate. Let me spell it out for you so that I'm sure you understand what I'm driving at.

You know of what Canaan is a type. Canaan isn't a type of heaven. Dr. G. Campbell Morgan used to tell us that if Canaan is a type of heaven, the first thing we should do when we get there is to drive out the Hittites, the Perizzites, the Amorites, the Canaanites, the Girgashites, the Jebusites, and all the other "ites." No, it is not a type of heaven. But it is a type of the place God has for His believing child, the life to which He is leading us on.

God's purpose when He saved us was to lead us on, that we might be conformed to the image of His Son. God is ordering our pilgrimage, if you will, from Egypt to get us into Canaan, but a lot of us have been unwilling to go. And a lot of us have never reached the place of God's plan for us in life for the selfsame reason Israel never got there. The Scripture is perfectly clear; for there are listed for us in 1 Corinthians 10 the five reasons Israel did not get to the place of God's appointment for them. We are not talking about heaven. We are not talking about salvation. We are talking about God's place for us on earth. I want to look at those five reasons, and I pray God's Holy Spirit will speak to your heart about them.

In the first place, we are told they lusted after evil things. Though I had read it many, many times, I turned back to the Old Testament to read the story again in Exodus, in Numbers and in certain chapters of Deuteronomy. As I looked at the things for which they lusted, and I was looking for that word *lust,* I was amazed to find that the things for which they lusted were necessary things, were useful things, were things that they absolutely needed. They needed food, and they lusted after food. I said, "Lord, why, why would You speak of lusting after evil things? Certainly these people in a wilderness journey needed sustenance." And God began to speak to me and it seemed to me that I was right in coming to the conclusion that food became more important to these Israelites than God was, that food became more important than the will of God. They were putting secondary things first, and first things second, and God said they lusted after evil things. Food in the desert became more important than going on to the land flowing with milk and honey.

So many of us who name the name of Christ are piddling away our time, terribly concerned about things that pass away. I wonder if deep in your soul—and I don't ask you to do what I haven't done and what I'm not willing to do tonight—but I wonder if deep in your soul you are satisfied? God has saved us to take us on, to lead us out, and we've said *no* because security and safety and food and relatives all mean more to us than the will of God.

They lusted after evil things, and I remind you that a day came when they wanted to change, when they would have given anything to have altered their decision. God said *no! No!* I'm sure here is the explanation of why I as a pastor wept before God because my people would only go so far with God and no further! They had gone far enough, and they missed out in all that God would do for them and in them and through them. They said *no,* and God said, "All right, it is *no.*" They lusted after evil things.

In the second place, the Israelites were idolaters. I certainly don't have to spell out for you that idolatry in the New Testament sense of the term is to put anything or anyone in the place of God. When John said to the Christians, "Little children, keep yourselves from idols," I'm quite sure he didn't have in mind that they needed instruction to keep away from the grotesque images that the heathen worshiped; they had turned from them. But there are other idols, and some of you have those other idols.

Perhaps some of you have gone to your pastor or some Christian teacher or leader and you've said, "Why is it that God doesn't use me more? Why is it that I can't go on further than I am? Why is my life so seemingly useless?" I think very often you will find the reason is some idol. When God says that we are to yield ourselves to Him, He means exactly what He says. When the Lord Jesus taught about discipleship and said that a man could not come after Him unless He hated father and mother and children and wife, He meant what He said. Compared to our love for Him, our love to loved ones should be as hate.

Have you an idol? Oh, don't keep saying *no* to God! God help you to tear the idol from His throne and worship only Him.

The third thing that this passage tells me is that Israel committed fornication. The reference makes clear that we go beyond Kadesh-barnea here, because the pattern of life set up prior to Kadesh-barnea has its consequences after Israel left there. So the incident of Baal-Peor is brought to our attention, that awful scene that was instigated by Balaam, the prophet, who, when he could not curse God's people, suggested to Balak that he provide an opportunity for the men of Israel to have intercourse with the women of Moab, and God's judgment fell upon them.

The sin of uncleanness—Baal-Peor. Says the Word of God, "Neither let us commit fornication, as some of them committed, and fell in one day three and twenty thousand." Oh, you say, if God were to act in judgment like that today, how many would be slain, for we live in a day of utter uncleanness and defilement? But wait a moment, wait a moment! How many, who can tell how many, have been set aside in the death of unusability in the hands of God because of this sin today? How many a young preacher, bright with prospects, has tampered with this sin and has gone down into oblivion. Talk about twenty-three thousand in a day! This is one of the sins that made God say *no* to His people.

The fourth sin related in 1 Corinthians 10 is that they made trial of the Lord. The reference is to another incident after the decision at Kadesh-barnea. The people were discouraged because of the way, and their souls loathed the manna that God had provided for them. So God sent fiery serpents among them. You know the story. Deliverance came only to those who looked upon the brazen fiery serpent made by Moses and lifted up in the camp. They made trial of God. They became discouraged in the way and they said, "Well, there is no use going on; the way is too hard." But the way they were going was the product of their own decision actually. They failed to believe God. I wonder if some dear preacher, some dear missionary, is in the same situation. You're discouraged because of the way. God said *no* to His people because they didn't believe Him.

And the final item is that they murmured. Oh, they constantly murmured! They wanted the onions and the leeks and the garlic of Egypt. They wanted to be in graves in Egypt. They wanted to be dead rather than living to go on with God. Utterly discouraged and complaining and murmuring against God. Do you recall the story of Kibroth-hattaavah, "the graves of lust"? There they died. Could God prepare them a table in the wilderness? Surely He could, but they didn't go on with God. So I want to lay upon your heart the tragedy of continually saying *no* to the will of God for your life, lest God should seal the decision as He did with Israel.

Oh, that something of the fear of the Lord would begin to get hold of us. You can't trifle with God and get off scot-free. He's not a kindly grandfather that you can kick in the shins and who laughs and says, "Do it again." God is holy! God is righteous! God keeps His word. It is a terrible thing to say *no* to God. God's warnings are not to be rejected with impunity. While the child of God, truly saved by grace and born of the Spirit and washed in the blood, has eternal life, I remind you he can become a castaway, he can lose his reward, he may be saved by fire—and that is a tragedy, a stark, naked tragedy, and it is an insult and a dishonor and an act of infamy against God's Son who loved us and gave Himself for us.

Don't you see, if God's warnings are to be no more than good advice, what is the use of them? And if they are more than good advice, they must have some teeth in them, and I want to say they do. Some of us have some decisions to make and we better start meaning business with God. We may have some people fooled, but God isn't fooled. We can fritter away our time so long, we can major or minor so long, we can demand our own way so long that God will confirm our decision and He will say *no* to our going on.

God says these things were our examples. Oh, you say, "It can't happen to me." What about Ananias and Sapphira? What about Demas? What about Alexander? What about Diotrephes? What about Lot? What about Sampson? What about Saul?

My friend, it's about time you stopped playing fast and loose with God. For though the grace of God is free, I remind you there is the discipline of grace, I remind you there is a government of God. Especially the child of God isn't going to sin wittingly and flagrantly and get away with it.

Has God said anything to you tonight? Has He? I don't know what it may be, but perhaps somewhere in this list of five sins of ancient Israel on the way from Egypt to Canaan is the thing you've been saying *no* to God about. Will you quit saying *no*?

Back in the days when I was a pastor, I very frequently would say to my people, 'You know, if there were just twelve of us who would really mean business with God, who wouldn't sit back on our oars and say, 'We're the people, we've arrived, we've gone further along than some of the others,' but who would have a divine discontent in our souls and we would really mean business with God, the ends of the earth would feel the impact of our lives." When they used to look at me rather incredulously, I'd say, "You doubt it? May I remind you that God used eleven men to turn the world upside down years ago; poor men, uneducated men, but men who had sold out to God!"

I'm speaking to some young man tonight, to some young woman who has said *no* to God. I want you to say *yes*. I've tried faithfully to warn you that you can keep on saying *no*, but you'll never get to the place God wants you to be where He can use you to defeat the giants that oppose God's people. Say *yes* to Him tonight.

1960

Claims Christ Made for Himself

AT THE OPENING of this Founder's Week Conference for 1960 I would like to draw your attention to some of the scriptures which unveil for us the wonder of the person of the Lord Jesus Christ, and I would in particular like to select some of the claims which the Lord Jesus made for Himself.

This day in which we live finds some men trying to distinguish between the Word of God and the Holy Scriptures. In the rush to propagate experiential religion, there are those who affirm that the sacred writings are the Word of God only when they have that content in the mind and heart of the hearer.

Now, Bible-believing people have acknowledged the necessity of receiving the sacred Scriptures and acting upon them as the Word of God if one is truly to profit by them, but they certainly have not taken the position that when such Scriptures are refused they are not the Word of God. After all, Bible believers know about man's stony, ignorant and sinful heart.

Passages like the following allow only one primary meaning, and their thrust is accepted by the believer:

> To the law and to the testimony! If they speak not according to this word, surely there is no morning for them (Is 8:20).
> Which things . . . we speak . . . in words which . . . the Spirit teacheth (1 Co 2:13).
> When ye received from us the word of the message, even the word of God, ye accepted it not as the word of men, but, as it is in truth, the word of God" (1 Th 2:13).
> If any man thinketh himself to be a prophet, or spiritual, let him take knowledge of the things which I write unto you, that they are the commandment of the Lord (1 Co 14:37).
> Men spake from God, being moved by the Holy Spirit (2 Pe 1:21).

> Heaven and earth shall pass away, but my words shall not pass away (Mt 24:35).
>
> For ever, O Jehovah, thy word is settled in heaven (Ps 119:89).

Certain theologians of the neoorthodox school brand such a concept as biblicism and claim that it is propositional rather than creatively renewed. But we reject any such idea, for it seems to us that such objection is merely a reflection of the old liberal concept of the evolution of religion.

As for the claims that the living confrontation of God's truth in history means the advance from error to truth and that it simply refers to the contemporary giving of inspired divine revelation, we deny both.

Concerning the first, the advance from error to truth, we believe that God's Word is truth. Concerning the latter, that is, the possibility of present-day revelation, we merely ask for the evidence of such revelation. I have not found anyone except liberals of the grossest sort suggesting other books to be added to the canon.

Moreover, the position of the neoorthodox theologian means that there is no absolute and final revelation of God. Not only may he be wrong, but he cannot possibly know finally if or where he is wrong, and such uncertainty certainly gives no rock upon which to build for time and eternity.

I would remind you that whatever the neoorthodox theologian thinks he has gained by adopting his view, we actually already have. For you see, the divine revelation is a living Word. There are certainly more insights into it to be found and there is further light to be broken from it, but it must remain the standard by which all other insights are judged. Let us not confuse the blundering of human opinion with divine revelation.

I would say finally in this connection that any such approach to this matter of authority in religion that leaves us without authority is rationalistic at heart. Men decide what is and what is not God's revelation—not on the basis of the testimony of the Bible to itself and in history, but on the basis of their limited experience, their prejudices, and their faults; and all of this happens with the master conspirator at large. Such a view, in my judgment, is the substitution of subjective speculation for the authority of Holy Scripture.

One of the places in which so-called propositional revelation is

CLAIMS CHRIST MADE FOR HIMSELF

most clearly explicit is that which concerns the person and work of the Son of God. Frankly, how else are we to know of this provision for man's redemption except in definitive statements given to us concerning our blessed Lord? Out of the many things the Word of God has to say about the Son of God, I should like to take just three things He said about Himself. These are simply three out of many.

I would remind you that He spoke of His preexistence. He claimed to be the Son of God and the Son of man. He identified Himself as the Messiah. He maintained that He was the Giver of the Spirit. He asserted that He is the Lord of the Sabbath.

But beyond these claims are three specific ones, which are not only historically true, but of tremendous importance for us today. There is, if you please, a living confrontation in history of these truths and they were never more important for men than now.

First of all, He claimed to be the indispensable Revealer of God.

> At that season Jesus answered and said, I thank thee, O Father, Lord of heaven and earth, that thou didst hide these things from the wise and understanding, and didst reveal them unto babes: yea, Father, for so it was well-pleasing in thy sight. All things have been delivered unto me of my Father: and no one knoweth the Son, save the Father; neither doth any know the Father, save the Son, and he to whomsoever the Son willeth to reveal him" (Mt 11:25-27).

The Son is not simply *a* Revealer of God, He is *the* indispensable Revealer of God and, according to His own claims, no man can know God except as the Son wills to reveal the Father to that one.

Think for a moment with me about eternal life. In essence, what is eternal life? Perhaps you suggest that eternal life is blessedness. I ask, whence this blessedness? That word *blessedness,* which denotes a joy and peace of heart and of being, may be descriptive of eternal life, but it is not a definition of eternal life. It is a result, it is a concomitant of eternal life, but it is not eternal life in essence.

You say, "Well, eternal life means heaven." But we already know that some would make a hell of a heaven if they ever got there, and we also know of others who have had a heaven in the midst of sordid circumstances. While certainly heaven is involved in eternal life, eternal life is something deeper.

It seems to me the Lord Jesus laid His finger on the true and foundational significance of eternal life when, in praying to His Father, He uttered the words recorded for us in John 17:3: "And this is life eternal, that they should know thee the only true God, and him whom thou didst send, even Jesus Christ."

Eternal life is in knowing God, in a personal relationship to God. Circumstances being what they may, though we look forward to the promises of God that involve heaven and His presence forevermore, the gospel song writer was not wrong: "Where Jesus is, 'tis heaven there." The presence of the Lord Jesus in the heart of the believer ought to guarantee heaven on earth, for eternal life consists essentially in this: that a human being knows God.

Now, of course, it is impossible for the finite fully to comprehend the infinite, I understand that. But there has been a revelation, there has been a disclosure, there has been an unveiling. While there are certain facts about this great God given to us in nature and given to us in the Word of God, the crux of the matter, the heart of the matter, is here, that the Lord Jesus is the indispensable and final Revealer of God, and if you are to know God, you must know Jesus Christ.

That is a far cry from what we hear in the world about the Lord Jesus. It is a far cry from what we hear certain so-called Christian preachers saying about the Lord Jesus. But this is His claim: "No man knoweth . . . the Father, save the Son, and he to whomsoever the Son willeth to reveal him."

May I emphasize the latter part of Matthew 11:27—"he to whomsoever the Son willeth to reveal him." Here is sovereignty, here there is complete authority—the Lord Jesus claims for Himself the absolute essentiality of knowing God through Him. Whatever may be said for other religions which deny the Lord Jesus, whatever may be said concerning their ethical standards or their specific and special insights, the fact remains that if this word of Jesus Christ is true, (and it is), the devotees of these religions do not know God.

Listen to the Word of God in John 5:23, "He that honoreth not the Son honoreth not the Father that sent him," and 1 John 2:23: "Whosoever denieth the Son, the same hath not the Father: he that confesseth the Son hath the Father also."

Our blessed Lord makes a claim for Himself that is absolutely unique—He is indispensable to the knowledge of the Father.

Men may know something about God from tradition, from the Judaic-Christian culture; they may know something about God from other religious teaching. But to know the truth you must have the Bible, and to know the Father you must know the Son.

So the word that attaches itself in my mind as I think of this claim of the Lord Jesus is the word *sovereignty*. He stands as Lord —the Lord of life—and to know God, and therefore to have eternal life, it is indispensable that you know Him. It seems to me that this claim of the Lord Jesus has tremendous importance for us today.

Do you know God—not merely in the statements of the Word of God about Him, which are essential to any true knowledge of Him, but in personal relationship, in which words have become living?

It is true, as the Lord Jesus said in John 6:63, "The words that I speak unto you, they are spirit, and they are life" (KJV).

The reality of God is not based upon the imaginations of man, not based upon the speculations of man, but upon the revelation of God, a revelation which concerns God's Son, who said of Himself, "No one knoweth the Son, save the Father; neither doth any know the Father, save the Son, and he to whomsoever the Son willeth to reveal him."

Do you know God? Do you have eternal life? If you do, are you thankful? Is there praise in your heart today that you know God? You see, the heart of hearts, the soul of souls, the spirit of spirits in this matter of eternal life is to know God and Jesus Christ whom He has sent.

The second tremendously important claim was that He is the Forgiver of sins.

There is a story recorded for us in Luke 5:17-26, which, by the Spirit, Matthew and Mark also record. I read it in Luke's account:

> And it came to pass on one of those days, that he was teaching; and there were Pharisees and doctors of the law sitting by, who were come out of every village of Galilee and Judea and Jerusalem: and the power of the Lord was with him to heal. And behold, men bring on a bed a man that was palsied: and they sought to bring him in, and to lay him before him. And not finding by what way they might bring him in because of the multitude, they went up to the house-top, and let him down

through the tiles with his couch into the midst before Jesus. And seeing their faith, he said, Man, thy sins are forgiven thee. And the scribes and the Pharisees began to reason, saying, Who is this that speaketh blasphemies? Who can forgive sins, but God alone? But Jesus perceiving their reasonings, answered and said unto them, Why reason ye in your hearts? Which is easier, to say, Thy sins are forgiven thee; or to say, Arise and walk? But that ye may know that the Son of man hath authority on earth to forgive sins (he said unto him that was palsied), I say unto thee, Arise, and take up thy couch, and go unto thy house. And immediately he rose up before them, and took up that whereon he lay, and departed to his house, glorifying God. And amazement took hold on all, and they glorified God; and they were filled with fear, saying, We have seen strange things today.

The story is an interesting one. You will recall it occurred in Capernaum. As this invalid was let down into the presence of the Lord, the Lord Jesus, recognizing the faith not only of the men who carried him but also of the man who was on the pallet, said a very strange thing: "Man, thy sins are forgiven thee." But the right of the Lord Jesus to say that was questioned by the official leadership of Israel, represented by the Pharisees and the doctors of the law from the villages of Galilee and Judea and from Jerusalem. They said, "Who has a right to forgive sins but God only?" The Lord Jesus didn't question that surmise, that conclusion, of these doctors of the law. Instead, He asked the question, "Why reason ye in your hearts?" and then further questioned them, "Which is easier, to say, Thy sins are forgiven thee; or to say, Arise and walk?"

I well remember as a boy reading this text and coming to the conclusion that it was easier to say, "Thy sins be forgiven thee," because no man could discover whether they were forgiven or not. But what the Lord Jesus is talking about is something more profound than that—to be able to say, "Thy sins be forgiven thee," and make it stick. To be able to say, "Thy sins be forgiven thee," and it is a statement of truth, is, of course, the more difficult. For in one way or another, certain of the sons of man, by the use of means, have been able to cure paralytics, but the sin question is in another realm and concerns matters which elude us and are too difficult for us.

For, you see, to face the sin question is to go to the root of the matter of our defection from God and all the train of sin that followed Adam's transgression. Put almost too simply, but spelled out in as short and as clear a definition as possible, the problem of salvation is simply this—how can a holy God meet with favor sinful man and restore that sinful man to fellowship with Himself —how can He do it?

This is the problem of redemption. Granted, God's heart is a heart of grace and a heart of love, yet a way must be found in which the holiness and justice of God shall not be outraged any more than that the grace and love of God should be shut up never to express themselves.

Some years ago I received a letter from a young theologian in one of the seminaries, asking me to express myself on a particular point. As is so often true of such individuals, he already expressed the point for me and all he wanted me to do was to say "Yes." The point he had in mind was that so far as my concept of the teaching of the Bible is concerned, I believed justice and holiness were the normative qualities in the character of God. He took the position that love and grace were the normative virtues in God.

It seems wrong to me to take an attitude of either/or in this matter. I take the position that the virtues of God, the excellencies of character of my God, are all normative and basic, and that there was in our God a disposition, a longing, a yearning to save men. I believe that with all my heart. Yet no one can ever raise a finger, point accusingly, and say that God's love was expressed at the sacrifice of His holiness and His justice.

There is a working together of these virtues of God, and so if the Lord Jesus is to forgive sins there has to be not only the display of the grace and love of God, but also the meeting of the requirements of God's honor involved in His holiness and in His justice.

So think for a moment—if the Lord Jesus is to forgive men their sins, then He must be able to satisfy the holiness of God; and to satisfy the holiness of God, He must Himself be utterly righteous. Moreover, He must be able to assume the guilt of man, and then He must be able to dispense the grace of God. In a word, He must have the capacity for infinite righteousness and infinite suffering if He is to save all who come unto God by Him.

However, for the Lord Jesus to claim that He could forgive sins, which He substantiated for the leaders of Jewry that day when He said, "But that ye may know that the Son of man hath authority on earth to forgive sins (he said unto him that was palsied), I say unto thee, Arise, and take up thy couch, and go unto thy house. And immediately he rose"—for the Lord Jesus to do that, there was a cross and there was a grave that had to be met.

So the word here that suggests itself concerning the person of our Lord is *infiniteness*. Let me put it simply. You and I are sinners; the wages of sin is death; the soul that sinneth shall die; and unless someone can take our place, the verdict of God cannot be circumvented. It is the gospel. Forgive me that I should seem to labor the point, but it is the blessed gospel. He died, "the just for the unjust, that he might bring us to God" (1 Pe 3:18, KJV). "Him who knew no sin he made to be sin . . . that we might become the righteousness of God in him" (2 Co 5:21).

Did you follow what I said? He must satisfy the holiness of God; He must be utterly righteous; He must assume the guilt of man; He must dispense the grace of God. But He must do it not for just one man; He must do it for all who come unto God by Him. That demanded infinitude.

Think of the tremendous claim that is here, involved in His right to forgive sins. It is on the basis of His giving His life a ransom for many that sins may be forgiven.

How important that word is to us today. Do you know the joy of sins forgiven? Are you thankful? I would not want to lay my head upon my pillow tonight unless I knew all was well between my soul and God, would you?

You *may* know, on the basis of faith in this blessed Saviour, who will say to you as He said to the paralytic long ago, "Thy sins be forgiven thee."

There is a final word from the Lord Jesus which I would like to draw to your attention, another tremendous claim. Look at John 5:22-23: "Neither doth the Father judge any man, but he hath given all judgment unto the Son; that all may honor the Son, even as they honor the Father. He that honoreth not the Son honoreth not the Father that sent him."

In the third place, the Son of God claimed to be the final Judge.

It would be absurd for me to make such a claim for myself, but the Lord Jesus made this claim—that all judgment is placed in His hands; that when men stand before the judgment bar of God, it will be the Lord Jesus they must face.

That He was speaking of the final judgment is made clear in the context, for He speaks of the resurrection of life and of the resurrection of judgment.

What is involved here? In one word, omniscience is involved here. For a man adequately to judge men, he must know the deeds which they have committed—the deeds done in the dark as well as in the light, in secret as well as in the open. More than that, he must know their thoughts; for man is responsible not only for what he has done, but for the thoughts he has harbored in his heart, which may or may not have brought forth actions. He must know the deeds of men; he must know the thoughts of men; but something even more difficult, he must know the motives of men. For even good deeds may plunge one down into abysmal darkness and worthlessness in the sight of God, when they have sprung from evil motives.

I submit to you, to know the deeds of men, to know the thoughts of men, to know the motives of men demands nothing less than omniscience. If the Son of God is to judge men, if He is to sit with nations before Him and divide them as sheep from the goats, He is the omniscient Lord. That is His claim—sovereignty, infiniteness, omniscience.

This matter of His being the Judge is of tremendous importance to us today, and I ask you the question, Are you ready to meet Him? Are you ready to meet Him as His servant at the judgment seat of Christ? Are you ready to meet Him if you are not God's child through faith in Him? (To ask that question is to answer it—you are not.)

These are propositional matters, but here is a living confrontation of truth today. This Lord Jesus is the indispensable Revealer of God, He is the Forgiver of sins, and He is the final Judge. The alternative to these claims is undeniable and clear. There is no logical alternative to the truth as the Lord spoke it, other than that He was demented or an impostor. Both these alternatives are unthinkable. But the bite is here. You cannot accept some of His teachings and dismiss others, and still call Him a good Man, an honest Teacher and a worthy Example.

Can you know God apart from Him? If you answer yes, you are on the opposite side from the Lord Jesus Christ—He said you cannot.

Can He forgive sins on the basis of His sacrifice? You say you do not like this reference to blood and a cross. All right, you are on the opposite side from the Lord Jesus Christ.

Is He the final Judge, or is judgment a figment of the imagination? If you say it is a figment of the imagination, you are on the opposite side from the Lord Jesus Christ.

These are some of the claims of the Son of God.

This morning I remind you of our glorious Lord. It is He who must bless if we are able to be blessed in this conference. It is He who must be honored if heaven is to come down, earth to bless. It is He who must speak if we are to have the opportunity to respond to the grace and power that He makes available.

Would you see Him this morning? See Him in His utter condescension as He left the glories of heaven to be born of a virgin? He was the object of the angels' praise and He departed from the place of glory. He walked out of the pearly gate and stepped down the azure-carpeted stairway of the sky to be born in a stable. See Him as He lived among men. The blessed Book of God struggles with limitations of human language to tell us of His perfections: "For such a high priest became us, holy, guileless, undefiled, separated from sinners, and made higher than the heavens" (Heb 7:26); "the only begotten Son, who is in the bosom of the Father, he hath declared him" (Jn 1:18).

If you would know the righteousness of God, look at Him. If you would see the love of God, look at Him. If you would understand God's attitude toward sin and sinner, behold Him. For he that hath seen Him hath seen the Father. To know Him is to know the Father, for He and the Father are one.

But behold how this glorious Lord stepped even lower than He had at Bethlehem. Marvel with me as the somber notes of His sorrow sound forth from Calvary. Do not pass it quickly—meditate upon it. "Him who knew no sin he made to be sin on our behalf" (2 Co 5:21). So on that cross of Calvary He died for us, but He arose and the bands of death were broken. By virtue of His death and resurrection He is able to save to the uttermost all who come unto God by Him.

His own arm brought salvation and His righteousness upheld Him.

He is the loving Saviour. Little children run to Him gladly. Helpless women find in Him the refuge of their souls. Strong men, lashed by the fury of the storms of life, seek Him as the shadow of the great rock in a weary land. He turns none away. He is the support of children, the help of youth, the guide of advancing years, and the strength of age. He is blessed, blessed Jesus!

There is one further vision of Him. He is coming again. He is the Judge, and in that assize that awaits the sons of men, He is the final Arbiter, He has the last word. To face Him, then, is tragedy indeed. No wonder men shall call for the rocks and the mountains to fall upon them—the strongest will shrink from that display of might.

Whatever your attitude toward Him now, in that day you will wish it had been to bow voluntarily; for you must face Him as a Saviour now, or as final Judge then. Then His eyes shall be as a flame of fire, and His feet shall be like burnished brass.

And so in His name I invite you, from your heart, to say with me:

>All hail the power of Jesus' name!
>   Let angels prostrate fall,
>Bring forth the royal diadem,
>   And crown Him Lord of all!
>
>Sinners, whose love can ne'er forget
>   The wormwood and the gall,
>Go, spread your trophies at His feet,
>   And crown Him Lord of all!
>
>O that with yonder sacred throng
>   We at His feet may fall!
>We'll join the everlasting song,
>   And crown Him Lord of all!
>
>   CHARLES WESLEY

May the Lord Jesus fill our vision in these days.

1961

Christian Joy

THESE ARE OMINOUS DAYS. I do not—I dare not—even seem to suggest otherwise. That God is trying to speak to all men, and especially to His children, is recognized by the spiritually sensitive soul. The message of this hour is clear. It is a clarion call for repentance, for faith, for discipleship, for courage, for exploits for God. May our hearts be quick to answer Him, may our wills be moved so that the proper action shall result.

However, for some reason known fully only to God, He has put another message on my heart for this hour. I trust that we shall see it to be not a contradictory word, but a complementary word. Lest our minds be troubled by undue perplexity because of terrifying world conditions, lest our hearts be overwhelmed because of all that which is coming upon the sons of men, lest our wills be petrified because of the potential dangers which beset each one of us, let me speak to you about Christian joy.

Joy? Who dares think of that word in an hour like this? If I need any vindication, I turn to my Saviour and listen to Him as He speaks in earth's darkest hour. For when the cross was but hours away, when the full import of all that He had come into the world to do, was readily apparent, I read that He said these words:

> These things have I spoken unto you, that my joy may be in you, and that your joy may be made full (Jn 15:11).
>
> Verily, verily, I say unto you, that ye shall weep and lament, but the world shall rejoice: ye shall be sorrowful, but your sorrow shall be turned into joy. A woman when she is in travail hath sorrow, because her hour is come: but when she is delivered of the child, she remembereth no more the anguish, for the joy that a man is born into the world. And ye therefore now have sorrow: but I will see you again, and your heart shall rejoice, and your joy no one taketh away from you. And in that day ye

CHRISTIAN JOY

shall ask me no question. Verily, verily, I say unto you, If ye shall ask anything of the Father, he will give it you in my name. Hitherto have ye asked nothing in my name: ask, and ye shall receive, that your joy may be made full (Jn 16:20-24).

Even in our Lord's high priestly prayer, this same theme reappears. "But now I come to thee; and these things I speak in the world, that they may have my joy made full in themselves" (Jn 17:13).

If the Lord Jesus could speak of joy in that hour, and if it was right and proper for Him so to do, I take it that it is not out of the will of God, it is not unscriptural, for us in an hour like this to remind ourselves of this subject of Christian joy.

Frankly, the Bible has a good deal to say about joy in sorrow. There is a paradoxical blending of grief and gladness, of sorrow and satisfaction, of bane and blessing. Granted, there are times in the Bible record when joy is the result of happy circumstances. I recall the story in 1 Chronicles 12 of the day when David was made king over twelve tribes of Israel. He had been crowned king of the southern tribes in Hebron seven and a half years previously. But now, at length, all Israel was to acknowledge his kingship. Gathered together, they anointed him king over the twelve tribes, and the divine record says, "There was joy in Israel" (v. 40). It was a happy occasion. The reason for the joy was manifest.

I recall as well a little later when David went to the house of Obed-edom to bring the ark of the covenant back to Jerusalem. You will recall that the record says they "went to bring up the ark . . . with joy" (1 Ch 15:25). There are those happy occasions when joy surely is right and proper in view of God's providential orderings and His great blessing.

Granted, too, that the Bible speaks of future joy. Recall the memorable words of Psalm 30:5: "Weeping may endure for a night, but joy cometh in the morning" (KJV). And the word in 1 Peter 4:13: "As ye are partakers of Christ's sufferings, rejoice; that at the revelation of his glory also ye may rejoice with exceeding joy."

Joy, the result of happy circumstances. Joy, in the future, promised and pledged by God. But there is at least one more way in which the Bible speaks of joy: it is joy in the midst of tribulation—

present joy even in adverse circumstances. Without reading the full context, indeed without even the full verse, let me call to your attention a series of passages which I think will effectively set before us this matter of joy in the midst of tribulation.

"I overflow with joy in all our affliction" (2 Co 7:4). What an amazing statement.

"Your faith . . . is proved by fire . . . ye rejoice greatly with joy unspeakable and full of glory" (1 Pe 1:7-8).

"Count it all joy . . . when ye fall into manifold trials" (Ja 1:2, margin).

In 1 Thessalonians 1:6-7 we read: "Ye became imitators of us, and of the Lord, having received the word in much affliction, with joy of the Holy Spirit; so that ye became an ensample to all that believe in Macedonia and in Achaia." You received the word in much affliction, with joy of the Holy Spirit.

No one can sincerely receive the Word of God, endeavoring to apply its principles and precepts to his conduct, without knowing what affliction is. There are material losses, shattered alliances, sufferings of body, struggles of soul. But whatever the suffering, there is the compensating joy of the Lord. Such gladness is not mere mental or emotional elation dependent on changing moods and influences. It is a deep and settled sense of God's blessing in the light of which every untoward experience loses its angry look and its power to disturb.

The joy of which I speak, the joy in the midst of tribulation, is profound. It is intense. It is serene, not boisterous. It stands in contrast to mere gaiety, merriment, mirth and pleasure. It is never aroused by trivia. It is always linked with wisdom, and always rests on the provision and promises of God. It involves contentment and satisfaction. It is steady and does not need to be transient. It is bliss, which is perfect joy.

There are just two matters that I wish to dwell upon in connection with this Christian joy that should be ours even in an hour such as this one. I would like to speak about the source of Christian joy, and then about the means of the communication of Christian joy.

Look with me, if you will, at Romans 14:17: "The kingdom of God is not eating and drinking, but righteousness and peace and joy in the Holy Spirit." The source of Christian joy is God. The

Holy Spirit is the one who creates and sustains joy in the heart of the believer. "The kingdom of God is . . . joy in the Holy Spirit."

Look at Galatians 5:22: "But the fruit of the Spirit is . . . joy." The product of the Spirit, the creation of the Spirit, that which the Spirit brings into existence, is joy. Oh, yes, I know the other eight virtues are there, but let me single out the one that is the object of our study and meditation, and so emphasize it. The fruit of the Spirit is *joy*.

It is interesting when reading the Word of God to discover how frequently there is reference to the believer's joy even in the most untoward circumstances. I turn to just one passage—Acts 13. At the close of the chapter, there is reference to Paul's ministry in Antioch of Pisidia. He had just preached a tremendous sermon. The Jews were pleased with what he had to say, and indicating that they wanted to hear him again, they left the meeting. The next week, when it became apparent that Gentiles as well as Jews were responding, the leaders of the Jews became jealous. They contradicted the things spoken by Paul and made it so difficult that it was necessary for the apostle to leave. I read in verse 50 that there was a persecution stirred up against Paul and Barnabas, and these men were cast out of their borders. As they went they shook the dust from their feet and went on to a place called Iconium.

But despite this difficult situation, despite the fact that these messengers of God had been sent away, I read in verse 52: "The disciples were filled with joy and with the Holy Spirit." Evidently they were able to see beyond the immediate circumstances, evidently they understood that God was on the throne, that God was working, and God had seen to it that the message had come to them; and somehow communicated to their souls was the joy of heaven, even in the difficult circumstances in which they found themselves. I point out that it is not just incidental that the verse says, "They were filled with joy and with the Holy Spirit," for the fullness of the Holy Spirit means also the fullness of joy.

This distillation of Christian joy in our hearts by the Holy Spirit is always miraculous. It is God's work; it is not of human origin. It is not a Pollyanna attitude toward life in which we try to kid ourselves that things are different from what they really are. It is not a joy based on circumstances that are favorable, pleasing to the flesh. It is a joy of divine creation. It is heaven born. It is from God.

Though it is true that it is always miraculous, may I observe that there is no mystery as to the reasons for or the means of the transmission of this joy. It is God's work in our hearts. He creates it. But He also has shown to us the reasons behind it, and the means by which it becomes real in our experience.

So think with me of the means of communication of Christian joy. In the Bible we see that there are at least two sources of the Christian joy that comes to us even in untoward circumstances.

First of all, there is that source which we may speak of as the special reasons why a child of God would have joy in his heart, whatever his circumstances. In the second place, there are the more abiding reasons, the permanent reasons, why the child of God should always have the joy of the Lord in his heart.

In regard to these special reasons, all we need to do is remind ourselves of some of the passages in the Word of God. We should certainly rejoice when others find the Lord. That is a special occasion. It does not happen all the time so far as our own individual experience is concerned. We don't see people being saved every second of every day. But we do see some who turn to the Lord and, when they do, there should be an echo, an answer from the depths of our hearts, to the joy in heaven over the repentance of one sinner (Lk 15:7). Acts 15:3, for example, says: "They [Paul and Barnabas] therefore, being brought on their way by the church, passed through both Phoenicia and Samaria, declaring the conversion of the Gentiles: and they caused great joy unto all the brethren." They were rejoicing that souls were saved. That is a special reason for thanksgiving, for praise to God, for joy in our hearts. God is saving souls.

Frankly, all of us should rejoice in the salvation of any soul, I don't care who leads him to Christ, I don't care what means are used. If the apostle Paul could rejoice that the gospel was preached even by insincere men—and he did (Phil 1:17-18)—certainly we can rejoice when the gospel is responded to and souls are saved. But watch yourself here. Just because God has used someone else to win that soul is no reason for you to be jealous and to lose the joy. God help us to rejoice in the salvation of souls regardless of whom He uses to win them.

Again, the child of God should have great joy in his heart when he sees Christians meaning business with God and growing in grace —going on in the things of God. That should encourage us greatly. Verse after verse comes to mind in this connection. I turn only to one. In Philemon 7 Paul says: "I had much joy and comfort in thy love, because the hearts of the saints have been refreshed through thee, brother." Here was a man who was living for God, who was ministering the things of God, who was being used of God, and Paul says, "There is joy in my heart as I see God's hand on you, as I see you responding to the leading of the Lord."

More than that, there is also the joy that God gives us—and I hope He gives it to us frequently—the joy of answered prayer. The Lord Jesus spoke of this, and I have already read it in John 16:24: "Ask, and ye shall receive, that your joy may be made full."

These are specific and special items brought to our attention in the Word of God, all of which should cause the joy of the Lord to overflow in our hearts and in our lives.

But there are also abiding reasons, abiding means for the communications of joy. I do not have to wait until I learn of someone's salvation in order to be joyful. I don't have to look around to see some child of God who means business with God and who is growing in grace in order to be joyful—though I certainly am. I don't have to wait until specifically and definitely I have an answer to prayer and say, "There is joy in my heart; God has answered my prayer." I don't have to wait for that. Though all these things are good and right, there are permanent reasons, abiding reasons. It is this matter which is upon my heart, the means which the Holy Spirit uses in creating and sustaining the joy of the Lord in our hearts. Let me suggest four of them.

First, there is the sense of God's presence with us. The mere contemplation of His person, of His care, of His provision, of His love and of His grace is enough to guarantee heart gladness for any child of God.

I venture to say, my dear Christian friend, that the reason for your disappointment, your discouragement, your despondency is that you have forgotten God! For I defy you to think upon Him and the revelation of Him, to think upon what He has done, and remain sorrowful. Contemplation of the person of God will mean that Christian joy will be in our heart, whatever the circumstances, whatever the testings, whatever the trials.

Mark it well, I'm not speaking of some ecstatic, emotional experience in which there is great outward display. I'm talking about the sense of bliss and of joy in the deep wells of one's soul. This, so far as the means of communication is concerned, is wrought by the Spirit of God as we remember who God is.

"God my exceeding joy" (Ps 43:4). "In thy presence is fulness of joy" (Ps 16:11). "I will joy in the God of my salvation" (Hab 3:18). "My soul shall be joyful in my God" (Is 61:10). "Thou shalt make me full of gladness with thy countenance" (Ac 2:28). "We . . . rejoice in God" (Ro 5:11). The reality of God—the sense of His presence, the realization of His goodness—is one of the means the Holy Spirit uses to create joy in my heart, to face any obstacles, to face any circumstances.

All of us surely have known Christians called upon to suffer great adversity, and somewhere you have met some dear Christian who, in the midst of it all, had the light of heaven on his face because the joy of the Lord was in his heart. It is so simple, isn't it? It is so simple we miss it. Have you met God this morning? Have you lingered in His presence? Have you waited long enough until something of the sweet perfume of His presence has covered you? This is one means God uses so that we shall be full of joy and of the Holy Spirit.

Let me give you a second means: the realization that God has spoken and that He enables us to understand His Word. Oh, my friend, it ought to be a constant marvel to us that the God of heaven, the omnipotent, supreme Lord of the universes, is so full of grace that He has communicated to you and me, that He has revealed His truth to creatures of the dust. God has given us His Word, and as we understand the marvel of God's grace in giving us that Word, and the additional marvel that He has made it possible for us, at least in some limited measure, to understand the message of the infinite, surely the joy bells of our hearts will begin to ring.

We have this, of course, many times in the blessed Book of God.

There is that interesting story in Nehemiah of the recovery of the book of God, the reading of it, and Ezra's giving the sense of it, as the people stood hour upon hour and heard the message of God. "Then he said unto them, Go your way, eat the fat, and drink the sweet, and send portions unto him for whom nothing is prepared; for this day is holy unto our Lord: neither be ye grieved; for the joy of Jehovah is your strength. And all the people went their way to eat, and to drink, and to send portions, and to make great mirth, because they had understood the words that were declared unto them" (Neh 8:10, 12). Somehow or other, it gripped them that day. God had spoken. God had revealed His will. They understood it and their souls were joyous!

I think it was something like this that was behind the statement of the psalmist in Psalm 119:162: "I rejoice at thy word, as one that findeth great spoil." It was a military man who wrote that, a man who knew well what it was to discover spoil, to take from the enemy his wealth, his resources. He said, "I rejoice in thy word, as one that findeth great spoil." Great advantage, great wealth, great prosperity is mine in the Word of God.

I think it was this same thought that was behind the expression of the prophet in Jeremiah 15:16: "Thy words were found, and I did eat them; and thy words were unto me a joy and the rejoicing of my heart: for I am called by thy name, O Jehovah, God of hosts." The Word of God—the reading of it, the believing of it, the understanding of it—this is one of the means the Holy Spirit uses to distill in our hearts the heavenly liquor of joy, of supreme joy, of eternal bliss!

There is a third avenue by which the Spirit of God brings into our hearts this joy. It is the consciousness that we have obeyed the Lord and that He is pleased. We have obeyed Him in believing on His Son. What was that word that the Lord Jesus said to the seventy disciples as they came back joyful that even the evil spirits were subject to them? The intent of His counsel was: Don't rejoice in that, rejoice in this: "that your name is written down in heaven."

Have you forgotten that fact? Oh, Christian, have the circumstances of life so borne in upon you and so inundated your soul that you have forgotten that God saved you? That will start the joy bells ringing. Yes, He did! Yes, He did! I was there when it happened, and I ought to know.

Not only is there joy that we have responded in obedience in believing in God's Son to the salvation of our souls, but may I suggest to you as well, there is joy in our hearts when, as Christians, we have obeyed His Word. There is that sense of oneness with God; there is that sense of God's approval that we have done what He has asked us to do.

One of the greatest servants of God in this respect was John the Baptist. There is a word recorded about him, a word that he said, which is a revelation of the Baptist as well, John 3:29: "He that hath the bride is the bridegroom: but the friend of the bridegroom, that standeth and heareth him, rejoiceth greatly because of the bridegroom's voice: this my joy therefore is made full." John heard Him. John obeyed God as the forerunner of the Lord. John experienced the joy of the Lord. If you would know this joy of the Lord in your heart, then walk humbly with your God. If you know what it is to be saved, don't allow any controversy between you and God to arise. The moment you do, joy is gone. The Holy Spirit communicates joy to the Christian heart that is obedient to the Lord.

There is a final word, a fourth means by which the Holy Spirit creates this joy in our hearts. There is the realization of that happy relationship for all who are born of the Spirit that we are members of the family of God. Don't you love to think about the family of God, or don't you think about it at all? There is something that happens in my soul when I contemplate God's family.

I remember—it has been years ago now, but the experience comes to me fresh every time I think of it—I was teaching the book of Ephesians to some of God's dear people in the East; I was their pastor. We had been going through some hard days and some of the dear Christians had been called upon to face great trial. We came to the prayer of Paul in Ephesians 3, beginning at verse 14. I approached this passage first of all trying to discover the outline of the prayer. What was on the heart of the apostle in this divinely inspired prayer that he made for these Christians? Although I studied the prayer carefully, somehow my heart was quickened, yet I did not have that sense of the presence of God, that freshness of a word from God that I knew my soul needed. I read verses 14 and 15 again: "For this cause I bow my knees unto the Father of our Lord Jesus Christ, of whom the whole family in heaven and earth is named" (KJV). The whole family! Somehow I understood for the first time in a personal, experiential way that it is a divided family, some are in heaven and some are on earth, but it is just one family. I know some up in heaven, don't you? We are still in the same family. They are in heaven; we are on earth, but it is one family, it is the whole family.

Oh, I'm glad I belong to that family. This gathering this morning transcends race; it transcends social distinctions; it transcends denominational lines! We belong to the family of God. God is our Father. And there is joy in my heart because that is true. If we are in Christ, we are in the family of God; and we are fellow members of the body of Christ and belong to that whole family in heaven and on earth.

As the Holy Spirit makes that truth real in us, the joy of God begins to bubble up in our souls. The spring of the fountain of divine truth begins to refresh our spirits, and the joy of God is a reality in our hearts.

I know I haven't exhausted the subject; but I hope that, even in an hour like this one, with all the foreboding word that comes to us from every part of the world, we shall understand anew that God wants us to have joy in our hearts.

What has God used most to refresh my soul and regale my spirit in life's darkest hours? I share with you the secret of my heart. It is the contemplation of God Himself. Henry Martyn, the great missionary, said, "My principal enjoyment is the enjoyment of God."

> Jesus, Thou joy of loving hearts!
>   Thou Fount of life! Thou Light of men!
> From the best bliss that earth imparts
>   We turn unfilled to Thee again.
>
> We taste Thee, O Thou living Bread!
>   And long to feast upon Thee still;
> We drink of Thee, the Fountain Head,
>   And thirst from Thee our souls to fill!

Bernard of Clairvaux in the twelfth century was saying what I'm trying to say in the twentieth century. The harrowing news from abroad, the evil portents that are involved in the imaginations of men and the threats of dictators, the sufferings of life, the troubles to which man is born as the sparks fly upward, should find us and leave us unafraid. The joy of the Lord is our strength.

1962

Singing to the Lord

> Let the word of Christ dwell in you richly; in all wisdom teaching and admonishing one another with psalms and hymns and spiritual songs, singing with grace in your hearts unto God (Col 3:16).

YOU ARE AWARE that singing is one of the few earthly exercises which will be perpetuated in heaven. There are many things we do down here that will not be continued in heaven. It is wonderful to have the opportunity of witnessing to someone about the Lord Jesus in order to win him to Christ. But can you imagine going next door up in heaven and trying to win someone to Christ? Bless your heart, he wouldn't be there unless he had already been won.

It is wonderful to get under the burden of prayer for some one specific request, some circumstance of life. Perhaps someone is sick, or a missionary may be in a place of great trial where discouragement has gripped his heart, or someone may be confronted with enemies that have the power, humanly speaking, to take his very life. Word reaches us and we bow together and meet at the throne of grace and we pray in intercession. Well, in heaven there won't be such circumstances, there won't be such enemies.

But there is one thing we shall have the privilege of doing in heaven that we have the privilege of doing on earth, and that is to sing. We shall sing the song of Moses and the Lamb.

Let us think together in a simple way about singing and about praising God in the Scriptures. You have noticed the prominence of song in the Bible. Someone has said that heathenism has no hymnbook. That is true. The heathen have their weird chants and their dirges of despair, but they have no joyful song. In striking contrast is the prominence of song in the Word of God.

There is the song of Miriam in Exodus 15. God had wrought for His people and opened the Red Sea before them. God had destroyed the enemies of Israel, and song was born in the heart of Miriam. She praised Jehovah, the God of Israel.

There is the song also of Deborah, because God had vouchsafed to Israel deliverance from the Caananites under the leadership of Barak. Sisera was dead and Jabin, the king of Caanan, was vanquished. In Judges 5, in a tremendous outburst of triumph, the victory song of Deborah is recorded for us.

There is the song of Moses, a little different in character, a little different in emphasis, found in Deuteronomy, beginning in the latter part of chapter 31 and continuing on through chapter 32. Bible teachers under whom I sat in my early days used to refer to it as the swan song of Moses, the word of praise and testimony to the faithfulness of God in which the resounding word of emphasis is upon God as the rock of His people. What a great song it is.

Of course I need not to refer to the songs of David, the songs of Asaph, the songs of the sons of Korah and others who were used of God to give us the Psalter.

May I remind you that the Lord Jesus sang with the eleven men He had chosen out of the world before they left the upper room, the night in which He was betrayed. It is recorded, "After they had sung a hymn they went out." I recognize what some of my brethren mean when they say they are glad they did not live in the time the Lord Jesus was on earth, because we have so many more blessings and we have His Spirit. But frankly, I would love to have been in that upper room to hear Him sing. I know what He sang. He sang the great hallel, Psalms 116, 117 and 118. I would love to have heard Him sing it. But I am going to hear Him sing someday, because Zephaniah 3:17 says He is going to sing.

I remember Paul and Silas sang. They were in prison in Philippi, and at midnight they were giving their praise to God in song. I suggest that that is the genius of Christianity. Anybody can sing when he is happy; anybody can sing when circumstances are all right according to worldly standards, but it takes a Christian to sing at midnight in the prison.

You see, the Bible is a book of song, and someday, the full open diapason of heaven's music will be heard and a new song will be sung. We read of it in Revelation 5:9-10: "Worthy art thou to take the book, and to open the seals thereof: for thou wast slain, and didst purchase unto God with thy blood men of every tribe, and tongue, and people, and nation, and madest them to be unto our God a kingdom and priests; and they reign upon the earth."

It is interesting to note, as well, that hymnologists have found hymn fragments in the Bible. It has been suggested that there are verses which might well have been sung by congregations that met in the name of the Lord Jesus in the early days of the New Testament Church. "Awake, thou that sleepest, and arise from the dead, and Christ shall give thee light" (Eph 5:14, KJV). Then that tremendous word of praise indicating who the Lord is and what He has done: God "was manifested in the flesh, justified in the spirit, seen of angels, preached among the nations, believed on in the world, received up in glory" (1 Ti 3:16, ASV). It is the rhythmical formation of such words in the original language that lead hymnologists to believe that here and there are fragments of songs of the early church in the Book of God.

I suggest to you that it is not an accidental occurrence that so much place is given to song in the Bible. It was Augustine of Hippo who delighted to remind his hearers that a new salvation demands a new song. The Bible is a book of salvation; therefore it is a book of song.

The second thing that I would suggest we think about is *who can sing*. I remember early in study of the Bible I came upon something. I was much more dogmatic about it then than I am now, but I still think there is a residuum of truth here that we ought not to pass by. Do you know there is not one place in all the Bible where the word angel is used as the subject of the verb "to sing." Now, I know about the reference in Job concerning the morning stars singing together, and I am willing to say angels can sing. I take it that they could sing better than some of us. I remember it was said about Lucifer before the fall that "the workmanship of thy tabrets and of thy pipes was in thee," and I take that to mean his voice was beautiful, that it was like an organ with pipes. So I don't doubt angels can sing, but it is an interesting thing that Scripture always says that the angels *said*. Even when the Gloria in Excelsis was given to the shepherds in the fields of Bethlehem, we read that the angels *said*, "Glory to God in the highest, and on earth peace, good will toward men" (Lk 2:14, KJV). It is just an interesting observation that the Bible does not seem to make much of the singing of angels, though they may well sing and sing as beautifully as creatures could ever sing.

But the Bible talks about redeemed men and women singing. "Let the word of Christ dwell in you richly; in all wisdom teaching and admonishing one another with . . . songs." It is those in whose heart the Word of God dwells who sing, and only those who know the Lord could be said to have the Word of God in their hearts. Actually, this scripture suggests that the Word of Christ is at home in their hearts. It is not only that they have memorized some Scripture, but the Word of God is at home in them, because there is a correspondence between the way they live and the way the Word of God says they should live. The Word of Christ dwells in them. These are they that sing.

Notice the end of Colossians 3:16 makes this plain: "Singing with grace in your hearts to the Lord" (KJV). And who can have grace in his heart except those who are God's children? We have received of the grace of God, grace upon grace, and we have been saved by grace through faith, "and that not of yourselves, it is the gift of God" (Eph 2:8). So Colossians 3:16 is saying to us that it is those who know the Lord, who know what the grace of God means in reaching lost sinners and saving them, those in whose hearts the Word of God dwells, who are exhorted in the Word of God to sing. The Word of Christ has found hospitality in our hearts, the grace of God has been received and accepted if we have responded to the gift of God's grace, and so we sing.

Another word—*Why do we sing?* First of all, we sing in praise to the Lord. What does the text say? "Singing unto God." For the Word is: "Teaching and admonishing one another with psalms and hymns and spiritual songs, singing with grace in your hearts unto God." Our hymns of praise, our hymns of worship are hymns of worship and praise to our God. This is a fitting way to come into the presence of the Lord, with praise on our lips as the reflection of the praise of our hearts.

I wonder if we remember this scripture when we sing our hymns of praise. There are hymns in which we are not singing to one another, and even though there were not another human ear to hear, it would make no difference; the hymn is a hymn of worship, of adoration, of praise. Look at just one of them with me. Take your hymnbook and put it right by your Bible. That is a good combination. You read the Word and let God speak to you; you pray to Him, and then it is wonderful to take a hymnbook and just read the hymns. This is a hymn of adoration, a hymn of worship and praise. It is an old hymn, which comes to us actually from the twelfth century, written by Bernard of Clairvaux.

> O Jesus, King most wonderful!
> Thou Conqueror renowned!
> Thou Sweetness most ineffable,
> In whom all joys are found!

You can pray that hymn. It gives expression to thoughts in my heart that somehow I haven't been able to find words to express. Listen to these stanzas:

> When once Thou visitest the heart,
> Then truth begins to shine,
> Then earthly vanities depart,
> Then kindles love divine.

And again:

> Thy wondrous mercies are untold,
> Through each returning day;
> Thy love exceeds a thousand-fold,
> Whatever we can say.

You see, alone before the Lord we can utter these words, for here is a hymn of worship and of praise to God. The first purpose of our song should be to praise the Lord.

But there are hymns that have other purposes. A hymn may be a testimony and a witness to someone who hears it and may even lead him to inquire about the faith.

We have already referred to Paul and Silas in jail. They were in the innermost prison, having been beaten, which means their backs were bloody. They were put in stocks, which means they were cramped and held in one position, their feet and hands being bound. Yet in that condition and in that place, which, of course, would have been a vermin-infested dungeon, they began to sing. What effect do you think that had on the jailer and on the prisoners? Those are very interesting words in Acts 16:25: "About midnight

Paul and Silas were praying and singing hymns unto God, and the prisoners *were listening* to them." I hear a lot I do not like to hear, but when I listen to something, I am giving attention. I don't think I am reading anything extra into this verse when I say one of the prisoners may have said to another, "Listen to those men. We know what they went through. We have been beaten with stripes, we have been in a dungeon, we have been in stocks; but listen to those men. Either they are insane, or else they have something we don't have. I am going to hear what they have to say." How did the jailer know enough to come to Paul and Silas and ask, "What must I do to be saved?" Where did he ever get the word *saved*. Don't ask me to prove it, but I think he heard them singing about it. You see, a hymn or a song may be a testimony or a witness to others, to fellow Christians or to the unsaved.

But it also may have as its purpose to build up Christian character and life. Did you notice that Colossians 3:16 speaks about "teaching and admonishing one another with psalms and hymns and spiritual songs"? In other words, there is a didactic purpose, teaching; there is an exhortation, an admonishing one another "with psalms, hymns and spiritual songs." In our use of "psalms, hymns, and spiritual songs," we should exhort one another.

There are hymns in which we teach one another. We can open our songbooks almost at random and find a teaching hymn. Look at the words of this hymn by Zinzendorf:

> Jesus, Thy blood and righteousness
>   My beauty are, my glorious dress;
> Midst flaming worlds, in these arrayed,
>   With joy shall I lift up my head.

What are we doing there? Reminding ourselves of the great truth that Christ died for us, and that the righteousness of God is ours through faith in the Lord Jesus. Therefore we can sing:

> Bold shall I stand in Thy great day,
>   For who aught to my charge shall lay?
> Fully absolved from these I am,
>   From sin and fear, from guilt and shame.

These hymns have a message, and the proper singing of them involves teaching and admonishing one another.

So I suggest hymns are used to praise God, to give witness to our experience with God, to develop Christian character and life in setting forth the teaching of the Word of God. Thank God, in this last area I have mentioned are the great hymns of comfort.

"Our Great Saviour" is a favorite of mine. Dr. J. Wilbur Chapman develops this hymn around one by Charles Wesley. Notice these lines: "Jesus, Lover of my soul." Look at the next stanza: "Let me hide myself in Him." The next: "While the billows o'er me roll"; the next: "While the tempest still is high," and the last: "More than all in Him I find." Dr. Chapman took those words from "Jesus, Lover of My Soul" and developed this beautiful hymn about the Lord Jesus.

> Jesus! what a Friend for sinners!
> Jesus! Lover of my soul;
> Friends may fail me, foes assail me,
> He, my Saviour, makes me whole.

That ought to do something to you if you are a Christian. It ought to make you stand up and even face the devil in the power of the blood of Christ and the power of the Holy Ghost. These hymns are hymns that teach us. They are not just words that we sing and then forget. How important it is that we should teach and admonish one another with psalms and hymns and spiritual songs. You see, the saints of God can be instructed and challenged and comforted by Christian songs.

What are we to sing? This verse in Colossians is almost duplicated in Ephesians 5:19, where we are told to sing psalms and hymns and spiritual songs. I recognize that diligent students of the Word of God have some question as to Paul's use of these three terms. Very early in the church the Psalter was used. The word *hymn* was used by the Greeks many years before the New Testament was written. It was used of a song which was addressed to a god. If it were addressed to a man, it was because he claimed to be a god, the emperor, for example. The early Christians had an abhorrence of this word evidently, because it is not found in any of the writings of the apostolic Fathers, presumably because of its heathen connotation. Paul, however, uses it in Colossians 3 and Ephesians 5. Certainly we know he was using it for praise to God, the God and Father of our Lord Jesus Christ, the true God.

So early in the church, a hymn came to be recognized as any sacred song that was addressed to God. Augustine said there had to be three things true of a hymn. It definitely had to be a song, it had to be praise, and it had to be praise to God. Whether that was true when Paul used the word, I cannot say, but I like this distinction. We can sing psalms; we can sing hymns, those songs addressed to God in praise, and then this third category, spiritual songs.

Certainly early in the history of the church these were songs of experience. Spiritual men sang spiritual songs. There were battle songs and harvest songs and festal songs and marriage songs, but these are *spiritual* songs. They have to do with the things of the Spirit, with the Word of God. Presumably one Christian is testifying to another Christian in a spiritual song, at least very early in the history of the church that was the meaning of this word.

Here is another matter that may interest you. The only word used for song in the book of the Revelation is this word, and transliterated into English it is our word *ode*. It is a spiritual song which indicates something of one's own experience in the things of God. "Blessed assurance, Jesus is mine! Oh, what a foretaste of glory divine" is an example. What are we doing? We are testifying of an experience with God, and the reality of it should give substance and sincerity and integrity to the song.

As I close, look again at Colossians 3:16: "Let the word of Christ dwell in you richly; in all wisdom teaching and admonishing one another with psalms and hymns and spiritual songs, singing with grace in your hearts unto God." I wonder how often you have sung that way in church? This is the scriptural teaching of how Christians ought to sing. Oh, that we begin to see that this matter of praise and of song is an integral part of Bible teaching. It is a great inestimable privilege that we can stand and praise our God and teach and admonish one another in the things of God, singing psalms and hymns and spiritual songs to the Lord. Though we may not be soloists, our voices together will create harmony and beauty as we lift our praise to God on high.

I plead for a return to a scriptural singing, for the praise and the honor and the glory of God. Let this forgotten exhortation be a remembered exhortation.

1963

Reflections on Some of the Ethical Implications of Certain Fundamentals of the Faith

"THE ORDINANCES of Jehovah are true, and righteous altogether" (Ps 19:9). Someone has translated this verse, I think appropriately, "The standards of Jehovah are true, and righteous altogether."

As I have been thinking about the ethical content of the Christian faith, my mind went out to some very obvious matters. I thought, for example, of the fact that the commands of Scripture to those who are the followers of the Lord are all ethical; they are righteous altogether, to use the language of Psalm 19:9. Perhaps they could be summed up in a phrase in Titus 2:12, where we are told to live "soberly and righteously and godly." I presume that each specific command of God with regard to conduct on the part of the child of God is subsumed under this threefold division: soberly, righteously, and godly. Soberly—my conduct personally toward myself; righteously—my conduct toward others; godly—my conduct toward God.

I thought as well of the fact, so far as the fundamentals of the faith are concerned—those which impinge particularly upon the life and ministry of our Lord on the earth—that each of these historical acts of God within time is itself ethical in the highest degree. You know, of course, that Christianity is a historic faith. By that we mean that it rests upon specific acts of God in history. Religions, as such, may simply be the rationalizations of men. They may be the codification of items of conduct. They may be the creation of mystic rites. But, in any case, the founder is never essential either to the origin or the continuance of the belief. Someone else could have founded it, could have originated the idea, and others have continued it.

But this is not so of Christianity. It is true that Christianity has its doctrines, its precepts, its philosophy; but at its center is Jesus Christ the Lord, and Christianity's convictions are convictions about Him. Christianity cannot exist without Him, for He is its center and its circumference. What He is and what He has done are the foundation of Christianity; and when I speak of the incarnation, or the atonement, or the resurrection, or the ascension, or the return of the Lord, I have spelled out either history or prophecy which has to do with actual historic facts—those events which have occurred or shall occur in the history of the world.

Now, all of these events in themselves are ethical. Let me suggest just one evidence. Take the matter of the incarnation: the delicacy with which that story is told, how carefully it is guarded from the sordid, and how it stands in graphic contrast to the stories of mythology about the gods and goddesses of the Greeks or of the Romans. There is nothing sordid about this story. God is operating in conformity to the principle of His own nature. He could operate no other way. Christianity in the historic acts which form the warp and the woof of this faith is ethical.

I thought, too, of the fact that the doctrines which are built on these historic acts and which grow out of them are likewise ethical. I suppose the superlative illustration of the rightness of Christian doctrine is no more graphically illustrated than in the biblical presentation of the atonement of our Lord and Saviour Jesus Christ. True, it is a stumbling block to the unbeliever. But to the individual who, touched by the Spirit of God, has had his eyes opened, the atonement becomes an amazing answer that God alone could give to the most serious problem ever to confront man. The problem, in short, is: How can a holy God meet and accept a sinful man and have that man fellowship with Him forever?

And God's answer to that question is not to lessen the demands of His holiness. Nor is it indeed to say that man's sinfulness is not as bad as it is. The unsullied holiness of God stands unbesmirched. The absolute total sinfulness of man stands in all its ugliness. But God has found the answer, and the answer is the invasion of God into the human family. An invasion? No, a coming in the likeness of sinful flesh. The Son of God was not sinful, but He came, according to Romans 8:3, in the likeness of sinful flesh. He became

Reflections on Certain Fundamentals of the Faith

a man and He lived without sin. He did no sin, neither was there any guile found in His mouth. But He died. Why did He die? He did not die for His own sins; He died for the sins of others. And God's answer to the sin question is the substitute Saviour, the Lord of glory who died for our sins according to the Scripture. Here is an ethical answer that protects the holiness of God and meets the sinfulness of man. Thus is the grace of God manifested. Thus is the love of God shown.

It was as I was thinking about these more obvious answers to the matter of the ethical character of the teachings of the Word of God that I began to think about some of the great truths connected with the Lord's life and ministry—the incarnation, the atonement, the resurrection, the ascension, and His future return. I became aware that there are implications for me in these historic facts. The New Testament doctrines involved in these five epochs in the life of the Lord have ethical implications for believers in Him. So I want to spend a while thinking about them with you. I shall select only one ethical implication for each of these epochs, one that has been most meaningful to me with regard to the conduct which is to be true of the child of God.

Let us proceed as logically as I know how, first by pointing out the historic fact in the words of Scripture; second, the doctrinal meaning of the historic fact; and then, the ethical connotation for the believer—what this fact and the doctrine based on it have to say concerning our conduct.

Let us start with the incarnation. In Matthew 1:23, one word, "Immanuel," God with us—the incarnation. In Luke 1:35, the angel speaks to Mary: "The holy thing which is begotten shall be called the Son of God." John 1:14: "The Word became flesh." Galatians 4:4: "God sent forth his Son, born of a woman." I have selected only four texts from many scriptures, but this is the historic fact: the Lord of glory was born of the virgin—the incarnation—God manifest in the flesh.

The doctrinal meaning of this? Surely it is simply that God became man, that the Lord Jesus is true God and true man. Apart from sin, He is as truly human as if He were not divine, and He is as truly divine as if He were not human. He is perfect Deity and perfect humanity in one person. Such a doctrine involves His preexistence and makes necessary His virgin birth. And while the biblical reasons for the purpose of His coming are many, the main reason is the redemptive one. "The Son of man came to seek and to save that which was lost" (Lk 19:10).

With the incarnation in view, what does that say to me, believing as I do in the revelation of Scripture and in the fundamentals of the faith? It certainly makes very clear one fact concerning the Lord Jesus Christ. It stresses His lordship and His sovereignty. That there are other truths also stressed, I do not deny—some very wonderful and comforting ones. But let me single out just this one because God has spoken to my own heart about this thing in unusual power and made it so irresistible that I must speak upon it. He is God. He is the Lord of glory. He is the blessed Son of God. And, as such, His lordship, His sovereignty, is unquestioned.

Here I am, a believer in Him. I believe in the incarnation. I believe that He is God manifest in the flesh. What does that say to me so far as my conduct is concerned? It says, I must obey Him. It is as simple as that, but it is tremendously important.

In Luke 6:46 the Lord is recorded as having spoken on this theme of His lordship in words which are the simplest in construction, for every word in our more common version is a monosyllable. "And why call ye me, Lord, Lord, and do not the things which I say?" It cannot be put any more simply than that. If He is Lord—and the Bible believer believes He is Lord and calls Him Lord—then, "Why call ye me, Lord, Lord, and do not the things which I say?" If He is Lord, then I never can say no to His commands. It is an anomaly for me to negate any positive command of His. For if I disobey while saying, "Lord," I am not acting in the light of His lordship; and of me it is true, as it was true of those of old, "This people draweth nigh to me with their lips, but their heart is far from me."

You see, this doctrine of the incarnation is not simply a theoretical idea that I must with force of will defend. It is not simply enough that I am adamant when the attacks against the deity of the Lord are brought forward. God help me to be that; I am not speaking against that. But I am saying there is something more, and the something more is that if He is Lord, then I can never say no to His command. If He is Lord, I can never complain about

His plan—at least I never should. Or, if He is Lord, I am His servant, I am His bondslave, and then it is His to say "do," and I do it; and "go," and I go. There can be no controversy; He is Lord. And if He is Lord, I should never doubt His love and I should never doubt His ability to get me home. He is the Lord.

I do not know what this does with you, but this begins to press William Culbertson. This begins to say to me that I am not my own, I am His, and the doctrine has its ethical connotation. Do not forget it. You say, "Well, I can prove the lordship of Christ in other ways." Certainly you can. This does not exhaust the subject; but, believe me, if this just begins the subject, it is a very good beginning. He is the Lord—the incarnate God—Immanuel.

Take the second of these doctrines, the atonement. For the historic fact, I again quote from only a few scriptures. I am embarrassed by the amount of Scripture which I omit. John 19:30: "He bowed his head, and gave up his spirit"; 1 Corinthians 15:3: "Christ died"; 1 Peter 3:18: "Christ . . . suffered . . . once, the righteous for the unrighteous"; 1 John 1:7: "The blood of Jesus his Son." The historic fact: He died; He shed His blood.

Now for the doctrinal meaning. Presupposing His lordship and His preservation from all taint of sin in coming into the world, and presupposing His sinless life as He came to the cross—all of which is true biblically—we come to His death. His lordship, His freedom from the taint of sin in coming into the world, and His sinless life provide the necessary basis for the acceptance of His sacrifice in the court of high heaven. And so we read, not simply Christ died, but we read, "Christ died for our sins" (1 Co 15:3). We read not only "Christ suffered once," but we read, "Christ suffered for sins once, the righteous for the unrighteous." We read not simply, "The blood of Jesus his Son," we read, "The blood of Jesus his Son, cleanseth us from all sin." We read, "Who his own self bare our sins in his body upon the tree" (1 Pe 2:24). You see, He could die for one other as the sinless man. He could die for all as the Lord who became man—the atonement.

What is the ethical connotation of the atonement? Behold, the sinfulness of sin! To save man, no less than the Father giving the Son was necessary. How heinous, how hateful, how odious is sin! Sin put my Lord upon the cross, and so the hatefulness of sin is an ethical connotation of the atonement. I ask the simple question, dare I love that which crucified my Lord? That the Son of God had to deal with human sin on the cross is God's answer to man's predicament—his lostness, apart from God.

But may I remind you that God's dealing with sin in this way in no way excuses sin. The Son of God, it is true, had to deal with human sin to effect forgiveness; but that in no way extenuates the sin or in no way grants license to continue in sin. Any such conclusion is sophistry of the worst sort. To truly enter into the historic fact of Christ's sacrifice and to love sin is utterly impossible. I am reminded of the word in Psalm 97:10, "O ye that love Jehovah, hate evil." I know of nowhere these feet of mine have stood and these knees of mine have bowed and this body of mine has been prostrate that has spoken more deeply to my soul than when in faith I bowed at the cross. "He loved me, and gave himself for me."

It was my privilege in 1952 to stand on the slope of Gordon's Calvary outside the Damascus Gate of old Jerusalem. I do not enter into the argument of the scholars as to the exact place where the crucifixion occurred. All I would affirm is that Gordon's Calvary to me is far more impressive as to what the scene must have been like than any place else I have seen. I remember I sought out the place where a cross could stand, and I stood there visibly moved. I bowed my head and the tears coursed down my cheeks. He loved me. He gave Himself for me. How can I longer continue in sin? How can I hold sin close to my breast as though it were my friend? How can I excuse my sinfulness? I opened my eyes. I looked at the ground and there, as though it were a sign from the Lord Himself to my own heart, bloomed three lovely crimson flowers. And I remembered, He shed His blood for me. How can I hurt Him? How can I grieve Him? "Shall we continue in sin that grace may abound? God forbid." God forbid.

Now for the third of these doctrines—His resurrection. The historic fact is found in Matthew 28:6: "He is risen"; in Romans 4:24-25: "Jesus our lord . . . was raised for our justification"; Ephesians 1:20: "He [the Father] raised him [the Lord Jesus] from the dead"; Luke 24:39-40: "See my hands and my feet, that it is I myself: handle me, and see; for a spirit hath not flesh and bones, as ye behold me having. And when he had said this, he showed them his hands and his feet." Hallelujah, Christ arose.

The doctrinal meaning? Our Lord came forth from the grave, first to prove the validity of His sacrifice. How do we know that what He did on the cross was accepted in the court of high heaven? We know because He arose from the dead; God has put His stamp of approval upon His sacrifice, for He is alive for evermore. He arose for our justification. Further, our Lord came forth from the grave to be the firstfruits of the resurrection, to be the token of glorious harvest. Again, our Lord came forth from the grave completely to overturn the power and authority of the devil. Revelation 1:17-18: "Fear not; I am the first and the last, and the Living one; and I was dead, and behold, I am alive for evermore, and I have the keys of death and of Hades." He is the mighty Conqueror.

The ethical connotation for believers? The possibility of triumph over sin. I read in Romans 6:4, "Like as Christ was raised from the dead through the glory of the Father, so we also might walk in newness of life." It is this mighty, transforming, powerful work of God—the miracle wrought when Jesus Christ the Lord broke the bonds of death and came forth triumphant from the tomb of Joseph of Arimathaea—that is the very basis of the possibility of our walking in newness of life.

> Risen with Christ, my glorious Head,
> Holiness now the path I tread.
> Beautiful thought, while walking therein:
> "He that is dead is freed from all sin."
>
> Walking, I'm walking in newness of life
> Free from the struggle and free from the strife;
> Trusting and resting and counting it done,
> Dwelling, I'm dwelling, the battle is won.

He is the Victor. The ethical connotation? The very possibility of walking to please God is involved in the doctrine of the resurrection of the Lord Jesus.

Look at the fourth doctrine—the ascension of our Lord. The historic fact, Luke 24:51, "While he blessed them, he parted from them, and was carried up into heaven"; Mark 16:19, "The Lord Jesus . . . was received up into heaven, and sat down at the right hand of God"; Ephesians 4:8, "When he ascended on high, he led captivity captive, and gave gifts unto men"; Hebrews 9:24, "Christ entered . . . into heaven itself, now to appear before the face of God for us." Forty days after the resurrection He led His disciples to the Mount of Olives, and while His hands were raised in blessing upon them, He was taken from them and received up into heaven. And the writer of the epistle to the Hebrews says He is there to appear before the face of God for us.

The doctrinal meaning of the fact? It is that the blessed Saviour in His resurrection body ascended into the presence of God, and He is there as our Mediator, as our Intercessor, as our Advocate. He is there waiting the day of His final triumph. He is there now, at the right hand of the Majesty on high. Blessed Saviour!

The ethical connotation? Let me select one scripture among others that God has been talking to me about recently concerning the preeminence of things eternal. Where do we get that from the ascension? Listen to Ephesians 2:4-6: "God . . . made us alive together with Christ . . . and raised us up with him, and made us to sit with him in the heavenly places, in Christ." That is where we are—at the right hand of God, in Christ.

In the light of that, let us read Colossians 3:1-2: "If then ye were raised together with Christ, seek the things that are above, where Christ is, seated on the right hand of God. Set your mind on the things that are above, not on the things that are upon the earth." We should be a heavenly minded people. That does not mean we are dreamers. That in no way teaches that with idle hands and complacent heart we should sit and rock our way through the world. It means that down here we should live with eternity's values in view. It means that our work down here should be fashioned in accordance with eternal values, not simply temporal values. For that which is seen is temporal, and that which is not seen is eternal.

You profess faith in the Lord Jesus. Let me ask you a question: For what are you living? For whom are you living? Oh that God would give us to understand so much we are living for is transitory and will be gone shortly. For "the world passeth away, and the lust thereof: but he that doeth the will of God abideth for ever" (1 Jn 2:17). That text summed up Mr. Moody's life. I have prayed in secret, "O God, somehow write that text in letters of fire upon the fleshy tablet of my heart; somehow register it that I shall never forget it, that I shall never attempt to evade it, and I will always live in the light of it." The Lord Jesus is in heaven. We are to live for heavenly things. The importance of eternal matters—an ethical connotation of the doctrine of the ascension.

One more thing—His return. The historic fact is voiced in prophecy and is just as sure as though it had occurred a thousand years ago. Acts 1:11, "This Jesus, who was received up from you into heaven, shall so come in like manner as ye beheld him going into heaven"; John 14:3, "I come again"; Acts 15:16, "I will return" (You thought MacArthur originated that?); 1 Thessalonians 4:16, "The Lord himself shall descend from heaven"; Revelation 19:11-14, "I saw the heaven opened; and behold, a white horse, and he that sat thereon called Faithful and True . . . and his name is called The Word of God. And the armies which are in heaven followed him." He is coming again.

The doctrinal meaning? Here is the vindication of the Lamb of God. Here He is claiming His crown rights. While we sing, "O that will be glory for me"—and that will be true—it is really, "O that will be glory for Him."

The ethical connotation for believers? One thing—there are many actually—but one thing, the thing that God has been talking to me personally about is in Revelation 22:12, "Behold, I come quickly; and my reward is with me, to render to each man according as his work is." What's the ethical connotation? Accountability. I am going to give an account someday. Second Corinthians 5:10 says: "We must all be made manifest before the judgment-seat of Christ; that each one may receive the things done in the body, according to what he hath done, whether it be good or bad." "We must all be made manifest." What does that mean? That means that everything is open and naked in the sight of Him with whom we have to do. That means that we will be stripped and stunned as we stand before Him, and life will be an open book and there will be no protestation we can make, no excuse we dare offer. We must all be made manifest before the judgment seat of Christ. And, dear friend, that day may come sooner than some of us anticipate.

These great doctrines that we love, that we stand for with all the enthusiasm and vigor that God can give us, these things for which we are set in defense, have ethical connotations. How obedient are you? How much do you hate sin? How much are you walking in newness of life? How much are you living for things eternal? How much are you living in the light of the accountability that is yours and which you will report at the judgment seat of Christ?

I love these doctrines—the incarnation, the atonement, the resurrection, the ascension, the coming again of the Lord—but each one of them has been talking to me about how I should live now—*how I should live now*. Hudson Taylor used to say, "There are two expressions that should be in the vocabulary of every Christian." I would like to add, I would be quite content if these two expressions were the whole vocabulary of every Christian. Listen to them: *today* and *that day*. God help us to live today so that we shall not be ashamed in that day.

1964

D. L. Moody's Life Text

IT IS ON MY HEART to speak to you on the text that moved a man whom God used to move the English-speaking world toward Himself. I'm thinking of Dwight Lyman Moody and Mr. Moody's text. Those of us who have had the privilege of standing by the graves of Mr. and Mrs. Moody on Round Top at Northfield, Massachusetts, know that there is inscribed very simply on Mr. Moody's tombstone his name, Dwight Lyman Moody, with the dates 1837-1899, and under these years, February 5, marking his birthday, and December 22, marking his day of entering into the glory land. There is nothing else on the tombstone except the quotation of part of a verse which his life exemplified so well: "He that doeth the will of God abideth for ever" (1 Jn 2:17). Turn to that text and let me read it in its entirety: "And the world passeth away, and the lust thereof: but he that doeth the will of God abideth for ever."

Mr. Moody, in 1855, turned from sin and self to the Saviour, and from that day as a young man until God took him home, the Lord led him step by step. He entered into an experience with God in which he sold himself out to the will of God, and it is no wonder that he would lay hold of a text like this and make it his aim in life. This text influenced his life. He believed it. He lived according to it. Will you think of some of the parts of it with me now?

"The world passeth away." In 1 Corinthians 7:31 we are told that "the fashion of this world passeth away." In one sense this demise awaits a coming day, for the eschatological Scriptures are clear as to the dissolution of the world as we know it. The Lord Jesus is recorded as having said in Matthew 24:35, "Heaven and earth shall pass away." The apostle Paul, writing to the Corinthians, said, "The things which are seen are temporal" (2 Co

4:18). Will you let these two texts linger in your mind and find lodgment in your heart, perhaps in a new way today?

"Heaven and earth shall pass away." "The things which are seen are temporal." That means that everything some people are living for is going to be obliterated. That means that what some people think is all that life contains, all that is worthwhile in our existence, will be gone, for the goal of their lives is the acquisition, the possession and the retaining of that which is material. "Heaven and earth shall pass away." Not *may* pass away—*shall* pass away. "The things which are temporal," the things which belong to the world of time and sense as we know them, these things are ephemeral, they will not last. The Word of God is clear and emphatic. So in one sense this passing away of the world awaits a coming day.

Perhaps it would be helpful to read another passage or two. Hebrews 12:26-27: "Yet once more will I make to tremble not the earth only, but also the heaven. And this word, Yet once more, signifieth the removing of those things that are shaken, as of things that have been made, that those things which are not shaken may remain." What is to be shaken? Not the earth only, but also the heaven. And says the writer of the scripture, as led of the Spirit of God: those things which are shaken will be removed.

Turn to 2 Peter 3:10-13: "The day of the Lord will come as a thief; in the which the heavens shall pass away with a great noise, and the elements shall be dissolved with fervent heat, and the earth and the works that are therein shall be burned up. Seeing that these things are thus all to be dissolved, what manner of persons ought ye to be in all holy living and godliness, looking for and earnestly desiring the coming of the day of God, by reason of which the heavens being on fire shall be dissolved, and the elements shall melt with fervent heat? But, according to his promise, we look for new heavens and a new earth, wherein dwelleth righteousness." Notice verse 10. The earth as we know it, the planet that we speak of as earth, says the Word of God, "shall be dissolved with fervent heat, and the earth and the works that are therein shall be burned up." Notice in verse 12, speaking of the heavens, "the elements shall melt with fervent heat." There is coming that climactic day in the economy of God when the Almighty will bring to destruction the earth and the world as we know it.

But may I remind you that 1 John 2:17 is not referring primarily to a coming day, but is speaking of the dissolution of the world as we know it currently, continuously, for notice the language, "the world passeth away"—*is* passing away. The emphasis here is on the present tense. You'll recall how the Lord Jesus rang the changes on this particular truth. Let me give you an illustration in Matthew 6:19-21: "Lay not up for yourselves treasures upon the earth, where moth and rust consume, and where thieves break through and steal: but lay up for yourselves treasures in heaven, where neither moth nor rust doth consume, and where thieves do not break through nor steal: for where thy treasure is, there will thy heart be also." The very materials which go to make up earthly life, these things have the mark of disintegration on them, have the sign of their obliteration written deeply upon them, for moth and rust consume, and thieves break through and steal.

The psalmist wrote of the destruction of earth and of life as you and I know it in Psalm 46:1-3:

> God is our refuge and strength,
> A very present help in trouble.
> Therefore will we not fear,
> > though the earth do change,
> And though the mountains be shaken
> > into the heart of the seas;
> Though the waters thereof roar
> > and be troubled,
> Though the mountains tremble
> > with the swelling thereof.

Thank God, we do not need to fear, but the fact is here that the earth does change. If there is one unchanging thing about the earth, it is its changeability.

Those of us who have grown older can look back and see how changes have transpired. What a disconcerting, discouraging thing it is to go back to the neighborhood where you were reared. The things that were brand-new are now old or are removed altogether. The familiar landmarks are gone. All the aspirations of your heart based on experiences long past seem almost to have dissolved with the material substances with which they were connected. The earth does change. The hymn writer was right:

> Change and decay in all around I see;
> O Thou who changest not, abide with me!

The world is passing away, and if we are trying to hold onto it, if we make it the object of our quest of life, if we try to satiate our souls by the gathering together of material resources of one kind and another, we are doomed to disappointment. The Word of God is clear—the world is passing away.

There is a second thing in 1 John 2:17. Not only is the world passing away, but we are told the lust thereof is passing away: "And the world passeth away, and the lust thereof." Now, I take it that the lust of the world has a threefold manifestation, for in verse 16 of this remarkable passage there is this word: "For all that is in the world, the lust of the flesh and the lust of the eyes and the vain-glory of life, is not of the Father, but is of the world."

This is an amazing text to me. I frankly have never gotten over the audacity of it which first reached me when as a pastor sitting in my study I was preparing to preach a sermon on "What Is Worldliness?" God spoke to me from 1 John 2:16. Think of it, "all that is in the world"—it doesn't say "some" of what is in the world. It doesn't say "a minimum" of what is in the world. It doesn't say "a majority" of what is in the world. It says "all." And God is saying to us, this is what the world has to offer in all its fullness; there is not a syllable to be added to it. This is the complete record of everything the world can offer any man, in any age.

And the more you think of it and the more deeply you dwell upon the words, you will come to this conclusion that God caused John to write this because it is the eternal truth. This is all the world can offer. The world can offer to satisfy your pleasure, to satisfy your appetite. It has those physical things which it can offer by way of ease and comfort and experience, the things we call pleasure—the lust of the flesh. I know I am speaking to some who are bartering away their lives for the pleasures of the world. God says they're there. The world can offer you pleasures.

Let's make absolutely sure that we understand that the pleasures of the world won't last, and that there will be a day of reckoning. I belong to an ancient generation. When I was a boy we used to hear a saying like this: "Sure, sow your wild oats." But "the morning after the night before" is another matter! I recall that there was a young man of whom the Lord spoke who asked his father for his possessions to go into the far country, and he went. The story of the prodigal son is so well known that I will not insult your intelligence by repeating it. I remember on one occasion hearing Dr. G. Campbell Morgan refer to the prodigal son, and he asked us a question which has lingered with me through the years. This great expositor said, "And where did the prodigal son get what he left home to find?" Where did he get it? He got it back home. That's where he got the sandals, that's where he got the robe, that's where there were the feasting and dancing, that's where there was the embrace of the father. The world cannot give you solid joys and lasting pleasure.

There is a second thing here: the lust of the eyes. The lust of the flesh appeals to our appetites, and the lust of our eyes appeals to our avarice and our desire for the acquisition of possessions. Perhaps you say, "I am not a fool, I am not dissipating the energies and strength of life in following the pleasure-mad throng. But I am going to secure the wherewithal to give myself that which I need to live." But possessions can become the supreme object of life. The world can offer you that. The lust of the eyes—some of you are living for that today, a house, an apartment building, a business building, stocks and bonds. I'm not saying these things are wrong, but I am saying that if all your life is centered in the acquisition of physical possessions, then the lust of the eyes has gotten the better of you, and that which the world can offer you, you have gone after. But like the rich fool, there will come the day when the Lord will say, "This night is thy soul required of thee; and the things which thou hast prepared, whose shall they be?"

It's so old I hesitate to tell this story, but it's so clear and relevant I must tell it. Two cronies met at the corner drug store, and one with baited breath whispered to the other, "Did you hear that Sam died?"

The other said, "No!" Sam was a sort of miserly fellow who was always trying to acquire more and more earthly possessions, and so the second man said to the first, "Sam's dead?"

"Yes."

"How much did he leave?"

And the first fellow said, "He left it all!"

Is that what you are living for, the lust of the flesh or the lust of the eyes?

There is one other thing the world can offer you and that is position, the pride of life, and vainglory of life. It can offer to satisfy your ambition so that you get to the top rung of the ladder and are able to order people about. The world can offer you that. And did you know that these three things are all that the world can offer? Some of us are selling our souls very cheaply, aren't we? Pleasure, possessions, position—the world can offer you these.

Now let's go back to 1 John 2:17. God is saying not only that the world is passing, but the lust thereof is passing away. One of the saddest sights I think I have ever seen is the individual who has lived only for the things of time and sense as he gets older and suddenly begins to realize he's not found life at all. There's a little phrase in Ecclesiastes 12 that haunts my memory and rises to challenge my soul again and again. Verse 5 reads: "And desire shall fail." The things that you think will satisfy will suddenly canker in your hands and turn into dust, and be blown away by the winds of the world.

D. L. Moody faced this fact that the world is passing away, and the lust of the world is passing away; and then he laid hold of the last part of the verse: "but he that doeth the will of God abideth for ever." Not he who doeth his fleshly will, not he who doeth the will of the world, but he that liveth according to the Word of God. All that the world offers is counterfeit so far as eternal satisfaction is concerned.

I was reading some time ago in the book of Proverbs and suddenly a verse leaped out of the twenty-second chapter that gripped my heart, for it shows the true source of satisfaction, and it shows it as over against what we have read in 1 John 2:16. Verse 4: "The reward of humility and the fear of Jehovah is riches, and honor, and life." "I want to live," says the worldling. "I want to give myself to experiencing the pleasures of the world." The Word of God says, "The reward of humility and the fear of the Lord is life." That's where life is. Riches are here. The answer to the lust of the eyes is not to be found in worldly pursuit, but in the will of

God. Humility and the fear of the Lord, indeed, are riches. And did you see the third word? "The reward of humility and the fear of Jehovah is riches, and *honor*, and life." If you want to live, if you want true riches, if you want enduring honor, then humble yourself before God, and walk in the fear of the Lord. Here is the answer to the human quest for riches, for life, and for honor; here is the true answer to man's hunt for pleasure, for possessions and for honor.

As I close I want to remind you that God has fulfilled His word to D. L. Moody. D. L. Moody laid hold of this—that he wasn't going to live only for the things of time and sense; he was going to seek the will of God, and God made the promise that he that doeth the will of God abideth forever. Of course, Moody will abide forever in heaven, but may I suggest to you that the influence of his life still abides. This comes very close to me; it comes close to my family, because one of my grandfathers turned to the Lord through the ministry of D. L. Moody, and the difference that made in the lives of his children and therefore of their children, and that includes me, has been profound. In a sense, any of us who have come to the Lord through the instrumentality of those who were reached by D. L. Moody are the living evidence that "he that doeth the will of God abideth for ever."

When I was the dean of the Institute, there came a letter from a United States soldier in New Guinea. It was very clear that he hadn't had the advantage of much formal training. Evidently a chaplain had slipped into his hands a book by Mr. Moody and it had this address on it, so he wrote to the Institute. As a matter of fact, he wrote to Mr. Moody, who died in 1899! The soldier said, "Thank you for your book on the love of God. It has helped me and I am living for God in New Guinea." Almost fifty years after Moody died, and the influence was still going on and going on. "He that doeth the will of God abideth for ever."

Let me give you one other illustration, and I could give you many more. In 1960, at the invitation of The Evangelical Alliance Mission, I had the privilege of going to speak at some of the biennial meetings of the missionaries as they gathered together to wait on God and to conduct their business. One of the places to which I went was West Irian, in those days called Dutch New Guinea. We were met at Biak by George Boggs of the Missionary Aviation Fellowship and flown over to Manokwari on the Birdhead. It was a real joy indeed to greet and to have the privilege of ministering to a number of those dear servants of God who had come in from over the mission fields of New Guinea.

When we finished our ministry there, it was arranged for us to go farther into the Birdhead into the Anggi Lake District. At that time the husband and wife who had been ministering in that field, and who had been used so notably of the Lord, were on furlough. So as we went into this little place, we found that there were only two young women on the station. One of them just a few years before sat where you sit, for she had graduated from Moody Bible Institute in 1958. She is a registered nurse, but she had her training biblically here at Moody Bible Institute founded by D. L. Moody. We had the privilege of spending an hour or so with Patricia Fillmore and her co-worker at the time.

The natives, hearing that the plane was coming, had gathered together a number of Christians and also a number of heathen. I was tremendously impressed that as these girls ministered to them it was very evident that they were loved by the people. The love of their hearts—even of the unsaved—was reflected on their faces and in their attitude toward the missionaries. It made an indelible impression upon us that these two women so sold out to God would minister in an area like that alone.

Just last month I had a letter from Patricia Fillmore. I want to read just a few lines from it. "Since your visit, the Lord has been working in hearts here at Anggi. About a year ago, the people started burning their fetishes or, as they call them, 'other gods.' That kept us busy collecting all the various things that they use for protection. Then Hank Bock burned them all in July. We had our first baptismal service in May, and then a few months ago approximately seventy more were baptized. Now there are about 140 in a new class." Need I say more, except: "He that doeth the will of God abideth forever."

Do you want your life to count for time and for eternity? Then sell yourself out to God. Have done with frittering away your time in the easy, pleasurable life which the world offers you and to which it beckons you, and begin to live for God. It is so true what Jim Elliot said, "He is no fool that gives up what he cannot keep to get that which he cannot lose." "The world passeth away, and the lust thereof: but he that doeth the will of God abideth for ever." D. L. Moody invested wisely—he lived both for time and eternity. Is it any wonder that when he was leaving this world he said, "I see earth receding [he had seen that for years], heaven is open, God is calling," and so he stepped from being the preacher of eternity into eternity, and the work has been going on ever since.

1965

What the Bible Demands If We Are to Understand It

We speak God's wisdom in a mystery, even the wisdom that hath been hidden, which God foreordained before the worlds unto our glory: which none of the rulers of this world hath known: for had they known it, they would not have crucified the Lord of glory: but as it is written,

> Things which eye saw not, and ear heard not,
> And which entered not into the heart of man,
> Whatsoever things God prepared for them that
>   love him.

But unto us God revealed them through the Spirit: for the Spirit searcheth all things, yea, the deep things of God. For who among men knoweth the things of a man, save the spirit of the man, which is in him? Even so the things of God none knoweth, save the Spirit of God. But we received, not the spirit of the world, but the spirit which is from God; that we might know the things that were freely given to us of God (1 Co 2:7-12).

I SHOULD LIKE to speak to you on the theme, "What the Bible demands if we are to understand it." A text which brings such a subject before us has been on my mind and heart for some time, from the eighth chapter of Acts—the story of Philip and the Ethiopian eunuch. "Philip ran to him, and heard him reading Isaiah the prophet, and said, Understandeth thou what thou readest? And he said, How can I?" (vv. 30-31). It is the answer to that question, "How can I?" to which I propose to direct our attention this morning.

At the outset, let me say that I am not suggesting that it is possible to comprehend fully all that is in the Word of God. With the psalmist I confess, "How great are thy works, O Jehovah! Thy

What the Bible Demands If We Are to Understand It

thoughts are very deep" (Ps 92:5). But I would remind you that it is possible to have some understanding of the Word, and I would observe that for most of us it should be greater than it is.

But I have another matter on my heart which I believe the Lord wants me to speak of today. There is a good deal being said, written and done that makes out as though the Bible were merely a human book that can be understood and explained merely by human investigation. The article in "the double issue" of *Life* for December 25, 1964, is for the most part notorious in this respect. The same idea seems inherent in the attempt by scholars, widely differing in faith, to formulate a common version for all these faiths. This project seems to say that a translation is merely a mechanical procedure. All you need is a group of scholars who have the knowledge and vocabulary, grammar, history, and some sympathy with the general import of what is said in the Scriptures. But what does the Bible itself say? What are the requirements which it demands? Thank God for scholars who have given us the Word of God in our own language. We do not make light of this gift. But we still insist that the Bible has some requirements which even scholars must meet if they are to understand God's Word. It will do us all good to look at these demands.

The Bible has its stipulations. Not just anybody can understand it. That everybody cannot understand the Bible is not because it is mystical, esoteric or cryptic. It is not because it is necessary to look for hidden meanings. It is not because it contains irrational statements, although there are mysteries beyond our comprehension. Infinite revelation to finite minds is bound to present difficulties. But an understanding of what may even be termed the elementary teaching of the Word of God is denied those who fail to meet the Bible's demands. What are they? Let us list some of them.

With the understanding that there will be some overlapping, there are broadly at least five such stipulations the Word of God makes for its own understanding. The first of these is the necessity of *salvation*. By salvation, I mean a salvation which involves the new birth. The Lord Jesus said to Nicodemus, "Verily, verily, I say unto thee, Except one be born anew, he cannot see the kingdom of God" (Jn 3:3). At this point the Lord Jesus did not say he cannot *enter* the kingdom of God. He said that later in verse 5. But in verse 3 He declares the kingdom of God cannot even be *seen* unless a man is born anew. "Now the natural man receiveth not the things of the Spirit of God: for they are foolishness unto him; and he cannot know them, because they are spiritually judged" (1 Co 2:14). A man not knowing what it means to be saved, not having been born again, is by the Bible's own definition incapable of understanding its revelation, for he doesn't understand the things of the Spirit of God. The apostle Paul in Romans 8:6-7 lays down the principle: "The mind of the flesh is death; but the mind of the Spirit is life and peace: because the mind of the flesh is enmity against God; for it is not subject to the law of God, neither indeed can it be."

The utter impossibility of that which is flesh understanding that which is spirit is, it seems to me, fully demonstrated in these quotations from the Word of God.

Now, in this matter of salvation, faith is an inherent part—faith in the Saviour. I trust that those hearing my voice this morning have long since made a decision to turn from their sins to the Saviour, that you know what it means to be a child of God—not by the world's definition of the term, but by the biblical definition. "As many as received him, to them gave he the right to become children of God, even to them that believe on his name" (Jn 1:12).

There is no shortcut; there is no way around. Salvation is necessary to enter into the meaning of the Word of God. Faith, then, is involved in this transaction—faith placed in the Son of God who died and rose again that men might be saved.

Faith that God has spoken is also involved. The God who spoke through the prophets has "at the end of these days spoken unto us in his Son" (Heb 1:1-2). There is a revelation. The Bible claims to be that revelation. It claims to have been brought to us by holy men who were moved by the Holy Ghost. It claims that it is the product of inspiration, the inspiration of God. "Thus saith the Lord" occurs again and again on its pages. So we believe that God has spoken.

By faith I do not mean, as is sometimes proposed, a leap in the dark. Faith can be rationally satisfying. For when we posit the God of the Scriptures, the possibility of divine revelation is established. Furthermore, from that vantage point, the whole revelation of what God says concerning God, man, sin and eternity ties together and makes exquisite sense. Granted, there are mysteries and we get beyond our depth, but there is no questioning the great essentials of our faith.

Involved also in this necessity for salvation to understand the Word of God is what the Bible speaks of as the creation of the new man. "Put on the new man, that after God hath been created in righteousness and holiness of truth" (Eph 4:24). That new man created by God has the capacity to understand God as we are taught by the Spirit of God.

Salvation is absolutely necessary to understand the Word of God. May I simply observe, how can men who make light of the gospel, the necessity of the shed blood of our Lord, the reality of His resurrection, have faith in the Saviour? Therefore what they say contrary to the Scriptures should not influence one who knows God in salvation.

In the second place, the Bible itself makes as one of its demands if it is to be understood, that the individual who opens its pages and pores over its message be characterized by *simplicity*. By simplicity I mean plainness, I mean artlessness, I mean humility, I mean unsophistication. I do not mean foolishness.

Listen to the Lord Jesus: "Verily I say unto you, Whosoever shall not receive the kingdom of God as a little child, he shall in no wise enter therein" (Mk 10:15).

In Matthew 11, immediately after our Lord has denounced certain cities that were given the inestimable privilege of hearing the Son of God Himself speak to them—Chorazin, Bethsaida, and Capernaum, we find that "at that season" (when in their sophistication, when in their worldly wiseness, when in their living wholly for the present, they turned away from the message of the Son of God). "Jesus answered and said, I thank thee, O Father, Lord of heaven and earth, that thou didst hide these things from the wise and understanding, and didst reveal them unto babes: yea, Father, for so it was well-pleasing in thy sight" (vv. 25-26). And that is still true.

In the recent issue of *Life* to which I have made reference, there is a quotation from a great scholar, Rudolf Bultmann: "I do indeed think that we can now know almost nothing concerning the life and personality of Jesus." On another page, a caption reads, "John's version is a puzzle to scholars." Strange indeed. I have known humble, unlettered souls whose lives have been transformed because they knew Him. I say no more. He has hidden these things from the wise and from the understanding and revealed them unto babes. Unless we approach Him in simplicity of heart, we shall forever remain in ignorance of Him and of what He can do.

The Bible's third demand, if it is to be understood, is the need for *spirituality*. First Corinthians 2, I think, makes this abundantly plain. "Things which eye saw not, and ear heard not, and which entered not into the heart of man, whatsoever things God prepared for them that love him" (v. 9).

Incidentally, that doesn't mean what a lot of people think it means. They think it has reference only to the things of eternity which we will discover when we shuffle off this mortal coil and go to heaven. That's not what it means. The emphasis is on things which entered not into the heart of *man,* things which *man* cannot discover, things which *man* cannot study out, things which *man* of himself cannot comprehend. The things you don't know as a *man,* you know as a *born-again man.* That is the emphasis. Notice, "Unto us God revealed them through the Spirit: for the Spirit searcheth all things, yea, the deep things of God" (v. 10).

The Spirit of God is not ours by virtue of our birth into the human family. Jude 19, a passage dealing with apostates, reads: "These are . . . sensual." The word "sensual" is exactly the same word translated "natural" in 1 Corinthians 2:14. The natural man cannot understand the things of the Spirit. He is limited to the things of time and space and is devoid of knowledge of the Spirit. He is earthbound. He is natural, not having the Spirit. And so I observe that the Spirit of God is not ours naturally.

In the second place, the Spirit of God is given to those who obey: ". . . the Holy Spirit, whom God hath given to them that obey him" (Ac 5:32). And when in obedience to the gospel, we turn from our sin and place our faith in the Saviour who loved us, who died for us, who rose again, not only are we saved, but part of that salvation is the gift of the Holy Spirit.

In the third place, *all* believers have the Spirit of God. "If any man hath not the Spirit of Christ, he is none of his" (Ro 8:9).

"Know ye not that your body is a temple of the Holy Spirit which is in you, which ye have from God?" (1 Co 6:19). And I remind you that this word was spoken to believers, even carnal believers. "Because ye are sons, God sent forth the Spirit of his Son into our hearts, crying Abba, Father" (Gal 4:6). All believers have the Spirit of God.

Fourth, the Holy Spirit is the great Illuminator of the revelation of God. Having given the revelation through holy men, He becomes the Illuminator of that revelation: "Ye need not that any one teach you; but as his anointing teacheth you concerning all things, and is true, and is no lie, and even as it taught you, ye abide in him" (1 Jn 2:27).

The anointing which we receive is the Spirit of God. He is the great Teacher. The conclusion I wish to reach in this matter is simply this: if we are to understand the Word of God we shall have to be taught by the Spirit. The Holy Spirit is the Illuminator of the divine revelation. So there must be an adjustment to the Spirit of God if we are to understand the Word of God. We must have Him, and we must be spiritual. Said the apostle to the Corinthian Christians, "I . . . could not speak unto you as unto spiritual, but as unto carnal, as unto babes in Christ" (1 Co 3:1). May I remind you that the first two syllables of the word "spiritual" are "spirit," and that is indicative of the fact that the Holy Spirit is essential and is central in all true spirituality. He, unhindered, unrestrained, must have the right of reign in our hearts if He is to exercise His function as Teacher. Then the Word of God will be open to our wondering view. Do you have these—salvation, simplicity, spirituality?

Fourth is the necessity for *study*. I read in the Book of God the motto of Moody Bible Institute: "Study to shew thyself approved unto God, a workman that needeth not to be ashamed, rightly dividing the word of truth" (2 Ti 2:15, KJV).

For though the Holy Spirit is the Teacher, and I make much of this truth, the fact of the matter is that He teaches us from the Book. Study, rightly divide. "Handling aright the word of truth," says the American Standard Version. What is that word concerning the righteous man in Psalm 1? It is this: "His delight is in the law of Jehovah; and on his law doth he meditate day and night" (v. 2). What was the word from Deuteronomy which the Lord used to repel Satan in the wilderness? "Man shall not live by bread alone, but by every word that proceedeth out of the mouth of God" (Mt 4:4).

I remember a quaint sentence in George Henderson's little book, *Exodus:* "The Bible is unlike any other book, in that one must personally know its Author before one can really understand its contents; it resembles other books in that to be understood it must be read; to be known it must be studied." There is no shortcut to an understanding of the revelation of God.

I would remind you that it is in this Book that God has revealed Himself and His will. We need this Book to correct our erroneous concepts and our partial insights into truth.

> To the law and to the testimony! If they speak not according to this word, surely there is no morning for them" (Is 8:20).
>
> He that rejecteth me, and receiveth not my sayings, hath one that judgeth him: the word that I spake, the same shall judge him in the last day (Jn 12:48).
>
> If any man thinketh himself to be a prophet, or spiritual, let him take knowledge of the things which I write unto you, that they are the commandment of the Lord. But if any man is ignorant, let him be ignorant (1 Co 14:37-38).

May I once again emphasize, perhaps unnecessarily for some, this matter of the humanistic approach to the Word of God, and the approach to the Word of God of one who believes in the supernatural. These are two opposite, entirely contradictory, and utterly opposing concepts. Actually, in this matter of whether the Bible is a divine revelation or whether it is man's quest for religious truth is the basic difference between the liberal and the fundamentalist. To the Bible-believer, the Bible is inspired by God, and it is indeed the truth of God's message for man; it is God's revelation of Himself, of man, of this world and the next. But, to the liberal, the Bible is largely, if not altogether, man's quest for religious truth. We as Evangelicals recognize that God spoke through holy men; God used men. The modernist's approach is that the Bible is merely a human record. The conservative accepts the testimony of the Book and of the Lord of the Book. "Men spake from God, being moved by the Holy Spirit" (2 Pe 1:21). "The scripture cannot be broken" (Jn 10:35). We must study that revelation.

What the Bible Demands If We Are to Understand It

It is not something that we invent. It is not something that comes out of a capacity of natural man, either to invent or to understand. It is a revelation from God. The Word of God understood, believed and obeyed means a life of joy and peace.

There is a fifth necessity, the necessity for *subjection,* submissiveness to God. It is not without meaning that in that tremendous chapter on yieldedness, on the appropriation of Christ as our life, Romans 6, that a passage is devoted to the theme of obedience:

> Thanks be to God, that, whereas ye were servants of sin, ye became obedient from the heart to that form of teaching whereunto ye were delivered; and being made free from sin, ye became servants of righteousness. I speak after the manner of men because of the infirmity of your flesh: for as ye presented your members as servants to uncleanness and to iniquity unto iniquity, even so now present your members as servants to righteousness unto sanctification. For when ye were servants of sin, ye were free in regard of righteousness. What fruit then had ye at that time in the things whereof ye are now ashamed? For the end of those things is death. But now being made free from sin and become servants to God, ye have your fruit unto sanctification, and the end eternal life (vv. 17-22).

Notice in verse 22, you became "servants to God"—or according to the margin, "bondservants." And so I go back to verse 16: "Know ye not, that to whom ye present yourselves as servants unto obedience, his servants ye are whom ye obey; whether of sin unto death, or of obedience unto righteousness." Willful disobedience to the known will of God will block your understanding of the revelation of God.

There were believers who chose to remain in carnality instead of going on with God. And what is carnality? Indulgence in the things of time and sense which rule out our out-and-out dedication to God. And a word had to be spoken to them. "When by reason of the time ye ought to be teachers, ye have need again that some one teach you the rudiments of the first principles of the oracles of God; and are become such as have need of milk, and not of solid food" (Heb 5:12).

Remember a parallel passage in 1 Corinthians 3 and understand that milk is the food of one who has not gone on with God, one who has been born again but has remained in infancy because other things occupy his attention and his heart. "Everyone that partaketh of milk is without experience of the word of righteousness." The thing God is driving at is not merely a theoretical comprehension of the revelation—it is an experiential realization in life of the meaning of that revelation. And unsubmissiveness and unyieldedness block the pathway to that which God is after—to conform you to the image of His Son.

And so here are five demands which I believe the Lord makes if we are to understand what He wants us to understand in the Book of God: *salvation, simplicity, spirituality, study* and *subjection*. Humble believers and learned scholars may know the Lord and the Book *if* they meet the conditions. Remember, the Bible makes its own demands as to who may understand it.

At Moody Bible Institute we love the Bible, we love the Lord of the Bible, and, God helping us, we'll remain true to the great fact that the Bible in the original autograph was the inspired, inerrant, infallible Word of the living God.

1966

The Foundation on Which We Stand

> For ever, O Jehovah,
> Thy word is settled in heaven
> (Ps 119:89)

THIS MORNING I should like to say some things about the Word of God. Most of them are probably well known to you, but I trust that in stirring up your pure minds by way of remembrance, your hearts will beat faster and your dedication will be made the deeper.

The doctrinal statement of Moody Bible Institute has a section devoted to the theme of inspiration. Article II reads: "The Bible, including both the Old and New Testaments, is a divine revelation, the original autographs of which were verbally inspired by the Holy Spirit (II Tim. 3:16; II Pet. 1:21)."

This statement includes at least four specifics. First, that inspiration is related to the Bible as a whole, which includes the thirty-nine books of the Old Testament and the twenty-seven books of the New Testament. Second, it involves the Bible as a *divine* revelation, and thus proscribes the modern unbelieving conception that the Bible is only a human document. Third, it specifies that it is the originals which may be spoken of as inspired in this sense; but let us understand that we have, to all intents and purposes, that Word before us today. And fourth, it clearly states that the kind of inspiration is verbal, that is, it has to do with words, not simply with ideas and not simply with the writer's gift of expression. This is Moody Bible Institute's doctrinal position in this matter of Bible inspiration, and we stand there today, as we have through the years past.

In view of this commitment, let me speak to three matters. Let me remind you first that this doctrine of inspiration is most certainly taught by the Scriptures themselves. Second, let me speak briefly concerning the history of this doctrine. And third, let me remind you of some of the reasons this doctrine is tremendously important.

First, the doctrine of inspiration is taught in the Scriptures. I am cognizant of the charge that to attempt to prove the Bible as the Word of God by quoting the supporting evidence from the Scriptures themselves is to reason in a circle, but let me make two observations. If the Bible itself denies its inspiration, then we would be utterly foolish to talk about it. Therefore, it seems to me we do well to see whether or not the Bible claims inspiration. May I also say that if the Bible remains silent about its inspiration, I think it would be difficult to maintain the doctrine. So my first observation is, let us see whether or not the Bible claims inspiration. My second observation is that there is corroborating evidence for the Bible believer and it supports the Bible's testimony. By corroborating evidence I mean such matters as the internal witness of the Holy Spirit to the Bible's truth; I mean also the external evidences, such as the power of the Bible, the durability of the Bible, the historicity of the Bible. All these, it seems to me, support the statement of the Bible itself that it is the Word of God.

It is impossible, of course, to mention in this passage all that the Bible says in this regard. What I have purposed to do is simply take a series of references that I think show clearly that the Bible claims inspiration again and again and again, and that it claims it for all its parts. Let us begin with Exodus 4:12, a word given by God to Moses. This is what God said: "I will be with thy mouth, and teach thee what thou shalt speak." According to this verse, I take it that what Moses spoke, and that which is recorded in the Bible as Moses' speech, was given to him by God. Leviticus begins (1:1-2): "And Jehovah called unto Moses, and spake unto him. . . . Speak unto the children of Israel, and say unto them," and God gave him what to say. This is the claim of the Word of God. In 2 Samuel 23:2, David speaks clearly: "The Spirit of Jehovah spake by me, and his word was upon my tongue." It seems to me the phraseology is evident, the claim is patent, the word is that this is God's Word. Moses and David so spoke.

Now go to the prophets. Isaiah 1:10 says: "Hear the word of Jehovah." I am informed that such a statement or the like occurs approximately twenty times in the book of Isaiah itself. In Jeremiah 1:1-2 we read in part: "Jeremiah . . . to whom the word of Jehovah came." Such a statement or its like appears almost one hundred times in the book of Jeremiah. Ezekiel 3:16 says: "The word of Jehovah came unto me." And approximately sixty times in the book of Ezekiel you will find that formula. Indeed, Zechariah speaks in 7:12 of Israel: ". . . lest they should hear the law, and the words which Jehovah of hosts had sent by his Spirit by the former prophets." So all the prophets before Zechariah are certainly spoken of as having given the words of the Spirit of God. Interestingly enough, when we come to the so-called minor prophets, such as Hosea, Joel, Jonah, Micah, Zephaniah, Haggai and Zechariah, all begin their prophecies with the declaration, "The word of Jehovah that came unto me," or words so similar that the difference is infinitesimal.

I am embarrassed by the wealth of such material which fell from the lips of the Lord Jesus. I will remind you of only one, John 10:35: "The scripture cannot be broken." Will you allow this one pregnant sentence to speak for the multitude of other references in which the Lord specified the same truth, "The scripture cannot be broken."

The apostle Paul by the Spirit of God in 2 Timothy 3:16 says: "Every scripture is inspired of God" (marginal reading). As you know, the literal translation is "Every scripture is God-breathed." Second Peter 1:21 gives Peter's testimony: "Men spake from God, being moved by the Holy Spirit." Then Peter reminded his readers in Second Peter 3:2: "Remember . . . the commandment of the Lord and Saviour through your apostles." So the commandment given by the apostles was the commandment of the Lord and Saviour.

Here we have a small compendium, if you will, of passages which show to us the claim of the Scriptures themselves. But, you say, there are problems in this matter, there are things that we don't understand, or there are things that seem to contradict other things in the Book of God. May I simply immediately acknowledge, certainly there are problems. Infinite revelation to finite minds is going to involve problems. If you think you have the pat answer to everything in Scripture, I would remind you that we are still on earth and we still do not know perfectly and fully. But it is my conviction that there is no problem for which a believing heart sooner or later will not find the answer, and a good answer, that will satisfy both the mind and the heart. I believe that what we know not now, we shall hereafter fully know and understand. "Then shall I know fully even as also I was fully known," says 1 Corintians 13:12. But what I do know now is so comforting and so powerful and so logical and so wonderful that I can trust the Lord with the rest. I therefore conclude point one by asserting that the Bible attests its inspiration, and that this claim is so widely spread throughout the Bible and is so all-inclusive in its application to the whole Bible that on its testimony we cannot logically believe in less than total plenary, verbal, full inspiration. Since it is God's Word, it follows that it is infallible and inerrant.

In the second place, let us consider the history of the doctrine, beginning with the Reformation. At that time, there was a twin battle cry that characterized the Reformers. The Latin designation involved in the battle cry was, "Sola fides" and "Sola Scriptura." By the former, they meant that salvation is by faith alone opposed to human works. The latter meant that divine revelation was restricted to the Holy Scriptures and was not to be predicated of tradition and of the edicts of the church. Faith alone and the Scriptures alone!

It was in the middle of the eighteenth century that unbelieving higher criticism began; and by the use of literary criticism and historical investigation, the inspiration of the Bible was attacked. We are now living in the time which liberal scholars call "the post-critical situation." The findings of these scholars of yesteryear are not to be disputed now, you see; they are to be meekly accepted, or else you are branded as an ignoramus. According to this view of liberal critical scholars, the Bible *may* contain the Word of God, but it is not that Word in totality. Indeed, some even suggest that it is false to call it the Word of God at all. In pious fashion they say that Christ is the only Word of God they know. But I should like to ask, how do they know what the Lord Jesus said? So far as I know, the only worthy record of His life and teachings is in the gospels, and, unless something happened overnight, they are still part of the Bible. Indeed, as a matter of fact, there is a third concept that some of these modern critical scholars hold. They claim that modern criticism has shown the gospels to be composed of various contradictory traditions so that it is impossible to believe in a historical Christ at all. Now they have gotten to the gospels and have done with the gospels what they did to the Pentateuch back in the eighteenth century. They have nothing to offer.

So much for this overview. Our concern, however, is that certain of these critical views are spreading. They have taken over some schools. They appear in magazines, both secular and religious; alas, in some religious magazines which were thought to be orthodox in the past. In short, there are not wanting signs of certain of them in evangelical circles. And as president of Moody Bible Institute, I want to sound again the word of warning. If we as orthodox, as Evangelicals, as fundamentalists, move from this doctrine, we are doomed to disaster.

That leads me to my third point, the importance of this doctrine as I view it. I take my stand, first, on the anthropological teachings of the Word of God concerning man naturally, and affirm that man needs divine revelation. If the Bible is not divine revelation, then we do not have that revelation in which we stand in need. Frankly, here is the basic cleavage between the liberal and the Bible-believing Christian. To the liberal, the Bible along with everything else is the product of evolution. Man is on an upward struggle for truth, and now we have outgrown the Bible. Having learned a little about God's creation, man thinks he has reached the point where he can speak authoritatively concerning the creation's Creator. And so some modern scholars have banished the God of our fathers and blatantly say the God pictured in the Word of God is dead.

Now, the Bible believer thrusts his sword directly at the evolutionary concept of continual progress in spiritual matters and asserts biblically that man needs divine revelation and divine life if he is to know the truth; and that, apart from Christ, man is sinful, twisted, and needs life. What says the Word of God? The Word of God affirms that the heart of man is desperately wicked (Jer 17:9). The Word of God tells us that "all have sinned, and come short of the glory of God" (Ro 3:23, KJV). The Word of God says that "the natural man receiveth not the things of the Spirit of God: for they are foolishness unto him; and he cannot know them"

(1 Co 2:14). Did you hear that? He *cannot* know them! However educated, however cultured, however gentlemanly, however accepted, *he cannot know them.* This is where we begin. The need for divine revelation, the need for the inspired, infallible, inerrant Word of God is first of all in the darkness and the twistedness of our natures. Men need—if they are ever to know the truth—the God-breathed Book, God's final revelation.

Second, if the Bible claims to be the Word of God and it is not the Word of God, then I say, it is a sham, a pretense, a hoax, and is not to be trusted at all. So let us not be so illogical as to disown the Bible as the Word of God, on the one hand, and then try to keep what we want of it, on the other hand. Oh, I know that man in his vaunted rational powers wants to make his choice of what to accept and what to reject. But, as we shall see, man's reason is a broken crutch that will afford him no ultimate good.

The third observation I should like to make as to the need for an inspired book is that, when all is said and done, man must still ask this question, By whose authority? Man must have a basis of authority or all is chaos. What is the voice that speaks infallibly? Where do I find what is right and what is wrong? How do I know what truth is as over against error? How can I know the meaning and the way to life now and hereafter? Who will begin to answer the questions that pound upon this mortal mind as I cry out for certainty, for some answer that will come across the ages and say, "This is the truth." By whose authority? It seems to me the crux of the matter confronting us—as I have viewed it in the message of the morning—is: Is it man's reason or is it divine revelation?

Now, you cannot be sure of man's reason. In fact, one of the strange things that perplexes my mind, as I think about it, is that the current brand of scholars is so certain of its conclusions, as though there will not be another brand of scholars in the next generation. I do not mean to be supercilious or cynical, but it seems to me that one of the marks of scholarship is to question the generation before. This may be all well and good within confines; but when it comes to the place where it repudiates the only divine revelation that we have, then it is time to speak, then it is time to stand on one's feet and acclaim loudly and emphatically our belief in the Bible as the inspired Word of God. Since you can't be sure of human reason, what is left to you? Without divine revelation, we must wander in the hopeless mazes of reason with no sure word from heaven.

The fourth observation I would like to make is this: that the doctrine of inspiration is basic to Christian teaching. All other doctrines stem from biblical inspiration and are supported by it. If the Bible is not true, then all the Christian doctrines go with it. For it is from the Bible's sacred pages that the truth, the hope, and the dynamic of life spring. The Bible has fashioned civilization as we know it. Western civilization is far from perfect, but its features of justice, of mercy, of human dignity come from the Bible. Rob us of the Bible, and where is morality and precept and power?

That leads me to my final point. The doctrine of inspiration is basic to Christian morality. Attack the Bible and you cannot long sustain the morality it teaches. You cannot question the Bible's integrity and preserve its morals. Indeed, for a long while we have lived on the faith and the foundations of our forefathers. Unbelief in the Bible was the exception in the nineteenth century. What there was of it was largely outside the church. Now men of little or no faith are in the church, and we wonder why our nation is in trouble. Economic prosperity has blinded us to our moral and spiritual poverty, but it is still true: "Righteousness exalteth a nation; but sin is a reproach to any people" (Pr 14:34). And it is still true: "The wicked shall be turned back unto Sheol, even all the nations that forget God" (Ps 9:17). The God some little men have the audacity to say is dead, isn't dead, and His Word abides.

Blessed Book, the Holy Bible! In it I hear the voice of my heavenly Father, the invitation of my gracious Saviour, and the tender pleading of the blessed Comforter. This Book unmasks my sin and convinces me of my need of the Saviour. It shows me the Redeemer in all the plenitude of His power, mighty to save, and I fall at His feet as His willing bondslave and worship Him. It comforts me in sorrow. It chastens me in disobedience. It strengthens me in testing. It encourages me in darkness. It makes faith grow in times of doubt. It is the gate of heaven to my weary soul, for in it I find that God speaks to the believing heart. It reveals to me God's provision to live as His son in a crooked and perverse generation, and thank the Lord for His miracle power in regeneration and sanctification. It shows me God's great plan that involves the completion of the church, the restoration of Israel, the putting down of sin and Satan, the vindication of God's Son and God's people, and the glorious enthronement of our blessed triune God, high over all. And I shout in answer, "Bring forth the royal diadem and crown Him Lord of all."

Blessed Book! The revelation of the heart, the will, the plan, and the provision of God for men, for you and for me. May our hearts beat faster and obey more quickly. This Book is God's loving gift, and it leads men to God.

So I end as I began: "The Bible, including both the Old and the New Testaments, is a divine revelation, the original autographs of which were verbally inspired by the Holy Spirit." Here we stand, so help us, God.

1967

The Offense of the Gospel

THE CHRISTIAN GOSPEL is the center and the circumference of Christian evangelism. There are other so-called gospels; we must beware of them. The true gospel not only gloriously answers the need of man; it also offends some men. The gospel is to be recognized not only by its wonderful content but also by its opposition.

In these days of ecumenicity when it is popular to discount our differences, it is in the interest of truth—if without bitterness or rancor—we point out the teaching of the Bible concerning the offense of the cross. May God help us from being personally offensive. May He likewise save us from toning down the distinctives of the Christian faith.

So let me say clearly, there are some things I do not believe.

I do not believe that the God of the Bible is dead.

I do not believe that there is no hell.

I do not believe everybody is going to heaven.

I do not believe in an ecumenicity that concludes everybody's religion is as good as anybody else's.

I shall respect each man's right to his faith or even lack of it. But that does not mean that I shall not attempt to convert him. I'll oppose any attempt to coerce him, or force him by physical or other means to a decision against his will. For I believe God wants only the glad-hearted, willing surrender of a heart to Himself.

Having said what I don't believe, let me change what I have said to what I do believe.

I do believe that the God of the Bible lives.

I do believe there is a hell to be shunned.

I do believe there is a heaven which men may enter if they come God's way.

I do believe in an ecumenicity among those who accept the Lord

Jesus Christ, who base their faith on the divine revelation of the inspired Scripture.

You may be aware of the fact that in some circles this belief that men are lost unless they know the Lord Jesus Christ as their Saviour is branded as intolerance, as bigoted, as narrow, and even as being against minority groups. Behind the repudiation of this teaching of Scripture that all men are lost is the idea that human brotherhood involves endorsement of other religions as legitimate and soul-saving. This I do not buy. I'll be a gentleman. I'll be friendly. I'll go out of my way to help those of other faiths, but I must not say that other faiths lead to God and heaven. And I deny that this is antiracial. It is religious, not racial. My love, for example, for God's ancient people and for men everywhere is manifested in the desire to help them physically and spiritually. I admit my kinship with them as "the offspring of God." I gladly confess my debt, especially to the Jew first, but also to the Gentile. But this does not mean that I must therefore deny the teachings of the Christian faith as taught in the Word of God. I believe that all men are sinners and that God Himself has provided the only way of approach to Himself.

All of this is forcefully brought to our attention in two passages which speak of the offense of the cross in the New Testament. The word "offense" in these passages is actually in the original the word from which our word "scandal" comes. It is the scandal of the cross. In its usage in the language in which the New Testament was written, in a very literal and common sense, it refers to a snare, a trap, and can quite legitimately be translated "stumbling block." It is so translated by the American Standard Version in the passages of Scripture to which I now refer. The first of these is Galatians 5:11, "But I, brethren, if I still preach circumcision, why am I still persecuted? Then hath the stumbling-block of the cross been done away." For the apostle Paul to have trusted in the rites of religion for his salvation would have delivered him from the opposition of many of his countrymen. Then the stumbling block of the cross would have been done away. But the apostle Paul refused any such escape from persecution. He did not preach circumcision. He was persecuted because the offense of the cross was something that he could not disown.

The Offense of the Gospel

The second passage of Scripture is 1 Corinthians 1:23: "But we preach Christ crucified, unto Jews a stumblingblock, and unto Gentiles foolishness." Let me read the context beginning at verse 18:

> For the word of the cross is to them that perish foolishness; but unto us who are saved it is the power of God. For it is written, I will destroy the wisdom of the wise, and the discernment of the discerning will I bring to nought. Where is the wise? Where is the scribe? Where is the disputer of this world? Hath not God made foolish the wisdom of the world? For seeing that in the wisdom of God the world through its wisdom knew not God, it was God's good pleasure through the foolishness of the thing preached to save them that believe. Seeing that Jews ask for signs, and Greeks seek after wisdom: but we preach Christ crucified, unto Jews a stumblingblock, and unto Gentiles foolishness; but unto them that are called, both Jews and Greeks, Christ the power of God, and the wisdom of God. Because the foolishness of God is wiser than men; and the weakness of God is stronger than men.

May I suggest two things about this passage of Scripture which deliver us from any bias that is merely natural and worldly. Notice in the first place that the whole race is involved in whatever condemnation is referred to in this passage, for Jews, Greeks and Gentiles are all mentioned—in verse 22, Jews and Greeks; in verse 23, Jews and Gentiles; in verse 24, Jews and Greeks. I take it that the Greeks are selected as the representatives of all the Gentiles, perhaps because of the emphasis upon their idea that the cross was foolishness, for the Greeks prided themselves upon their wisdom. In any case, whatever is involved in the condemnation of men, it takes in the whole race, not just one section.

In the second place, notice the two things which are specified—that to the Jews, Christ crucified is a stumbling block, it is a snare, it is something over which they stumble. This is merely a statement of fact. There is no opprobrium attached to it, save that they have divested themselves of the blessing that God otherwise would have given them. A stumbling block—all of us can stumble. Notice the second word, "foolishness," and this is the word which characterizes the Gentiles' attitude toward the cross.

I do not think it is difficult for us to enter into the meaning of these words and see them in their application. We have two men before us, representative of the whole human race. I think it would be fitting to call one a religionist; for not all Jews are involved in this category, just as all Gentiles are not involved in the category of those who brand "Christ crucified" foolishness. As a matter of fact, the opportunity for men to come to the Lord, to know the salvation of God, is open to both; because verse 24 says "unto them that are called, both Jews and Greeks." So there is no bias one way or the other. God is not a respecter of persons. The believing Jew and the believing Gentile are welcomed and made part of God's spiritual family.

It is true that many of God's ancient people in Paul's day were concerned about this matter of signs, which is mentioned in verse 22, "seeing that Jews ask for signs." I read in Matthew 12:38-40: "Then certain of the scribes and Pharisees answered him, saying, Teacher, we would see a sign from thee. But he answered and said unto them, An evil and adulterous generation seeketh after a sign; and there shall no sign be given to it but the sign of Jonah the prophet; for as Jonah was three days and three nights in the belly of the sea monster; so shall the Son of man be three days and three nights in the heart of the earth." You see from this answer of our Lord, while He certainly indicated that signs should not be necessary, He did not deny to His people a sign. The sign was this—that as Jonah was three days and three nights in the belly of the sea monster, so the Son of man would be three days and three nights in the heart of the earth. I take it that this refers to His death and to His resurrection. So the great crowning evidence that the Lord pointed to as the sign was His death and resurrection.

You will recall Matthew 16:1-4: "And the Pharisees and Sadducees came, and trying him asked him to show them a sign from heaven." And the Lord Jesus answered, "An evil and adulterous generation seeketh after a sign; and there shall no sign be given unto it, but the sign of Jonah." But it was a sign. That that sign was not enough to convince all doesn't argue against the fact that it was a sign; and for those who accepted it, they found what God offers to one who believes in the crucified and risen Saviour.

In John 4 a nobleman came to the Lord Jesus. The margin speaks of him as a king's officer. The Lord said to him, "Except

The Offense of the Gospel

ye see signs and wonders, ye will in no wise believe" (v. 48). And so the Jews seek for a sign; for somehow or other Christ crucified, the Messiah dying on a Roman cross, is unthinkable, it is utterly objectionable, it is a stumbling block. The New Testament gives its sad commentary, and I say it with great sorrow of heart, blindness in part has happened to Israel. Oh, that God's ancient people would see.

Now, having said that, putting myself in their place, sitting in their room, I think I can understand their confusion. They thought of the seed of Abraham in whom they would be blessed forever, but they forgot the seed of the woman who would be bruised in overcoming evil. They thought of the Servant of Jehovah who would be exalted and lifted up and made very high, but not of the Servant of Jehovah who was to be cut off out of the land of the living for the transgression of His people. They thought of the Shepherd of Israel who would lead Joseph like a flock, but not of the Shepherd of Jehovah of hosts, Jehovah's Fellow who would be smitten. Seeing the glories, they missed the sorrows, and have failed to comprehend that the sorrows lead to the glory. There is no harshness in my heart, there is not a trace of anti-Semitism in my soul. I love God's ancient people. They gave us the Saviour. Under God, they gave us the Book of God. It is my conviction that anti-Semitism is unscriptural and in its essence is against the God of the Scriptures. But this is the truth: Christ crucified is unto the Jews a stumbling block.

Unto the Greeks it is foolishness. Here is an amazing thing. Those who propounded the ideas that had shaped civilization for centuries, proud of their wisdom, failed to see in the cross the wisdom of God. You recall that little parenthetical word in Acts 17:21: "Now all the Athenians and the strangers sojourning there spent their time in nothing else, but either to tell or to hear some new thing." Always searching, always on the quest of truth, seeking knowledge, gathering information, showing a certain degree of wisdom. A great people were the Greeks. But the Greeks stumbled too. They stumbled because they saw in the cross nothing but utter foolishness to meet the needs of man. "Christ crucified . . . unto Gentiles foolishness," says 1 Corinthians 1:23. Let's think about this for a moment.

One of the hardest lessons I had to learn in my early ministry was why good, logical, moral citizens would brand the cross of Christ as foolishness, why they would speak of it as a medieval conception, as a slaughterhouse religion; for it seemed to me the most logical thing, the most wonderful thing, in all the world. It seemed to me that it was the answer to the sin question that only God could have propounded, that only God could have thought of. You see, I'm a sinner, and I know that sin separates me from God. I know that eternal death awaits the unrepentant sinner, and I need deliverance. However I may advance my education, however I may develop my culture, however I may be accepted among men, deep down underneath there is the sense of guilt, and of shame, and of condemnation; for God says, "The soul that sinneth it shall die," and "the wages of sin is death." I find myself unable to extricate myself from the pit of my lostness and my condemnation. But the good news is this, what I cannot do and what other men cannot do for me nor for themselves, God has done. God sent His Son, virgin-born, who without sin of His own bore my sin in His own body on the tree, and God says, "If you'll trust my Son, I'll forgive you."

"Oh," says the Greek, says the Gentile, "foolishness." Why is it foolishness to him? First of all, it is foolishness because of what we may call the mystery of it. Do you recall that when the inner veil of the tabernacle was woven in Old Testament times, cherubim were worked into the veil, and it is called "cunning work" in Exodus 26:31 and 36:35 (KJV). May I suggest that the cross is the cunning work of God. It is the answer to what I have just in simplicity tried to say, which in more theological language is termed the problem of redemption: how can a holy God meet and forgive and restore to fellowship sinful man? How can that chasm be bridged? God's answer is the cross. And if you refuse that cross, God has no other answer.

I recall sitting under a very wonderful teacher of theology who taught me much of appreciation for the great truths of the Word of God. Very frequently I heard him quote a verse that at first did not lay hold of my soul, but in its repetition over a long period of time it has come to be part of life for me. He spoke of Psalm 85:10 as having its greatest example and fulfillment at Calvary.

THE OFFENSE OF THE GOSPEL

Listen to it: "Mercy and truth are met together; righteousness and peace have kissed each other." How can mercy and truth come together? The truth is I'm a sinner, I'm lost, I'm under the condemnation of God. How can God be merciful? The answer is the cross. "Righteousness and peace." How can I have peace with God? I'm unrighteous. Righteousness demands my execution. The answer is the cross. It's the cunning work of God. It's God's answer to the sin question.

In the second place, the cross is foolishness to men because of what we may call the cross's imperialism. By that I mean its intolerance, its bigotry, its narrowness—you see, the cross says it is this way and no other. The broadminded, liberal man repudiates any such idea. This is obnoxious to him, it is repelling to him. I for one shall not alter what the Word of God says. Acts 4:12 declares: "And in none other is there salvation [speaking of Jesus of Nazareth, raised from the dead]: for neither is there any other name under heaven, that is given among men, wherein we must be saved." In 1 John 5:11-12, "God gave unto us eternal life, and this life is in his Son. He that hath the Son hath the life; he that hath not the Son of God hath not the life"; John 3:36, "He that believeth on the Son hath eternal life; but he that obeyeth not the Son shall not see life, but the wrath of God abideth on him." And the crowning words of all, the words of our Saviour Himself who would gather all unto Him: "Jesus saith unto him, I am the way, and the truth, and the life: no one cometh unto the Father, but by me" (Jn 14:6). Yes, it is the only way. But while it may be the only way, it is the way all may come if they will. Will you turn from your idea of the cross and take God's teaching, believe God's truth? You'll be surprised at what God does, for this is the way to new life. This is the answer to relationship with God. This is the answer to reality.

The cross is mystery. The cross is imperialism. But there's a third reason Gentiles reject the cross and brand it foolishness. It is this—its devastation of human pride. Every religion of the earth that I know about says, "Something in my hand I bring" as it approaches God. The New Testament faith alone says, "Nothing in my hand I bring." For all human effort, all of man-made works, has to be passed by. It is not by works of righteousness which we have done (Titus 3:5). It is by grace we have been saved through faith and that not of ourselves, not of works, lest any man should boast (Eph 2:8-10).

"Unto Jews a stumblingblock, and unto Gentiles foolishness." But if the message ended there I am sure I would not preach from the text today. The message ends this way: "We preach Christ crucified . . . unto them that are called, both Jews and Greeks, Christ the power of God, and the wisdom of God." I am glad once again to have the privilege as a preacher of the gospel to say, if there is any soul who will mean business with God and in honesty confess himself a sinner and turn to the Saviour who died and rose again, God will meet him and will transform his life, and God will lead him as he is willing to be led. That is the reason we can't give up in this matter of trying to convert people. Not because we want them miserable like we are, but because we want them to know the joy of the Lord like we do. In the words of the Lord Jesus we say, "If thou knewest the gift of God, and who it is that saith to thee . . . thou wouldst have asked of him" (Jn 4:10).

So I trust that as we think of these things, we see again the centrality of the cross, the tremendous importance of the cross, and the distinctiveness of the cross. And let us make sure we hold our banner high. I would be true, I would be honest, and this is what I believe the Scriptures teach. In this I take my stand, lovingly inviting all, Jews and Gentiles, to come, to believe and to rejoice in the Lord and the salvation of God. The word of the cross is unto us who are saved the power of God, says Paul in 1 Corinthians 1:18.

I know I'm speaking to someone to whom life is a burden. It seems that all the expectations of the years passed have gone down the drain and there's no satisfaction, and there's no life. You have form, you have ritual perhaps, but you don't have life. I invite you to turn to the Saviour and to trust in Him.

Some of you are wondering why I'm preaching the gospel. Well, God help me if I don't preach the gospel. Some of you are here to study the deep things of God, and you say, "You're dealing with the milk of the Word." I am. There are two emphases in Founder's Week this year: one, evangelism, and the other, the second coming of the Lord. We have mentioned the first of these already.

May God in this critical hour give us a new insight into our responsibility and privilege of being God's witnesses to the ends of the earth. God help us to move out in a new thrust of biblical evangelism ere the night come when no man shall work.

"Eloquent, rhetorical, philosophical preaching may inform the intellect, please the taste, appeal to the senses; it may even convict. But only the preaching of Christ crucified can save, can bring pardon, peace, justification and power."

1968
The Weapons of Our Warfare

IT IS ON MY HEART to speak on the theme, "The Weapons of Our Warfare."

There is a general recognition that these are ominous days. The great increase of knowledge is paralleled only by man's inability to harness it, so that we seem to be sitting on an atomic bomb that may explode momentarily. Somewhere I heard the story that when evangelist Billy Graham was ushered into the presence of Winston Churchill before the latter retired from active service, the great prime minister greeted him with this plaintive question: "Young man, is there any hope?"

Our world is a world of secularism, materialism, moral breakdown, international chicanery and conflict. Our own nation knows immorality in the forms of drunkenness, robbery, arson, sexual deviation, adultery, lawlessness, unbelief. These are dangerous days. These are days when courts hand down decisions which protect the rights of criminals over the rights of society. These are days when churchmen have denied the Book, traduced the Lord, endorsed sin, and now wonder why conditions are as they are. The Word of God is plain: "They sow the wind, and they shall reap the whirlwind" (Ho 8:7). Indeed, the text for our day may well be: "Because iniquity [lawlessness] shall be multiplied, the love of the many shall wax cold" (Mt 24:12).

What shall we do? We do not decry "positive action." We acknowledge the need for the worthwhileness of proper legislation, civil defense, police effort to fight crime. We do not oppose legal investigations. We do not oppose the efforts of good men to find panaceas. But what is our basic duty as Bible- believing Christians? What are we to do? There is injustice. There is mounting crime. There is a terrifying turning from things just decent, let alone the higher ethic of Christianity. Lawlessness is abroad. Fear grips

The Weapons of Our Warfare

many hearts. What are we to do? Are we to parade? Are we to demonstrate? Are we to get into politics? Are we to set up lobbies in Washington? Are we to do all we can within the law to protest wrong and champion the right? Whatever may be said for such activities, let us remember that these are not our chief weapons. They are not our strongest weapons. They are not our best weapons.

It seems to me that we need to remind ourselves that our chief enemy is not a man. And it is not a group of men. It is not a human organization. It is not an inimical "ism" that is our chief foe. Our chief foe is Satan, and his powers of darkness. "Put on the whole armor of God, that ye may be able to stand against the wiles of the devil. For our wrestling is not against flesh and blood, but against the principalities, against the powers, against the world-rulers of this darkness, against the spiritual hosts of wickedness in the heavenly places" (Eph 6:11-12). The conflict of the ages is going on. And let me observe that what is behind the lawlessness and moral breakdown in the world today is satanic in origin. Frankly, the Bible teaches that seducing and teaching spirits and demons are to lead men astray in later times (1 Ti 4:1). Our weapons, therefore, cannot be of this world. Buildings, worldly success, wealth, worldly acclaim, earthly authority will not avail. Our weapons have to be spiritual.

There is a parenthesis in 2 Corinthians 10 that goes to the heart of the matter and establishes the principle to which I would like to address myself now. Verse 3 reads: "For though we walk in the flesh, we do not war according to the flesh," and then verse 4 continues and is a parenthesis: "(for the weapons of our warfare are not of the flesh, but mighty before God to the casting down of strongholds)." Or, as another version has it, "the weapons of our warfare are not carnal, but are mighty before God to the pulling down of strongholds." We propose, then, to think with you of these weapons of our warfare which are not carnal but which are mighty, to the pulling down of strongholds.

What are our secret weapons? What can we lay hold of in order to make the greatest contribution, not only to the welfare of the church but to the well-being of society as well? I take it that there are at least six such weapons God has put at our disposal. It is not my purpose to deal exhaustively with these, but I should like to mention them, for all of us need reminding of these things. In what I shall say there is nothing new. But I think I shall be mentioning things that have been largely forgotten.

The first of these weapons of our warfare is the power of prayer. James 5:17-18 tells us: "Elijah was a man of like passions with us, and he prayed fervently that it might not rain; and it rained not on the earth for three years and six months. And he prayed again; and the heaven gave rain." If you have a marginal reference Bible you may see that a more literal translation of "he prayed fervently" is that "he prayed with prayer." I think the translators have gained the idea of that repetition, "prayed with prayer," for it denotes completion; it denotes fervency; it denotes earnestness; it denotes a literal laying hold of God. These are not simply words falling from Elijah's lips. These were words that tumbled over his lips from a fervent, warm heart that knew and loved God and believed that God heard and answered prayer. Elijah prayed with prayer.

I have given tribute on other occasions to the book on prayer that helped me most in my early ministry, *The Power of Prayer,* by a former leader of Moody Bible Institute, Dr. Reuben Archer Torrey. I have been reading it again, and I came to a passage comparatively early in the book I couldn't pass by. I want to read it for you now because it humbled me before God, it spoke deeply to my own soul about my own desperate need to learn to pray. Listen to these words from Dr. Torrey:

> I believe that the devil stands and looks at the Church today and laughs in his sleeve, as he sees how its members depend upon their own scheming and powers of organization and skillfully devised machinery. "Ha, ha," he laughs, "you may have . . . your costly church edifices and your fifty-thousand dollar church organs, and your brilliant university-bred preachers, and your high-priced choirs, and your gifted sopranos, and altos, and tenors, and basses, and your wonderful quartets, your immense men's Bible classes, yes, and your Bible conferences, and your Bible institutes, and your special evangelistic services, all you please of them, it does not in the least trouble me, if you will only leave out of them the power of the Lord God Almighty sought and obtained by the earnest, persistent, believing prayer that will not take 'no' for an answer."

"Prayer has as much power today," writes Dr. Torrey, "when men and women are themselves on praying ground and meeting the conditions of prevailing prayer, as it ever has had." Has God spoken to you recently about this matter of praying with prayer? Or have you been so occupied with things temporal, so seeking after outward demonstration of success, that the place of prayer is cold and empty.

Periodically God has spoken to my heart again and again from certain texts of Scripture. As I prepared to speak to you this morning, I asked Him to speak to me again from these passages. Listen to Isaiah 64:7: "There is none that calleth upon thy name, that stirreth up himself to take hold of thee." Oh, how God has excoriated this cold heart of mine about my prayerlessness with that text. For, you see, prayer doesn't come easily and naturally, and it isn't something we like to do in our fleshly natures. We have to stir up ourselves. And we have to mean business to lay hold.

Along with that verse I think of Acts 6:4 where the early disciples said, "We will give ourselves continually to prayer" (KJV). We'll give ourselves. It takes a bit of doing. It isn't something that comes automatically. We'll give ourselves—with purpose of heart, with determination. We'll give ourselves to prayer. Ephesians 6:18: "With all prayer and supplication praying at all seasons in the Spirit, and watching thereunto in all perseverance and supplication." And linked with that verse is Jude 20: "praying in the Holy Spirit." I remember hearing something like this: "We may be beaten in the conflict. We may be worsted in the battle. Our faces may be plunged in the dust of defeat, because of the power of the adversary and the greatness of Satan, but we're not beaten yet! For we can still lay hold of what John Bunyan used to call 'all prayer.'" And that's what Ephesians 6:18 is talking about—with all prayer and supplication, at all seasons, in the Spirit.

The simplist definition of praying in the Spirit came to me years ago from a great Bible teacher in the East, who said, "We pray in the Spirit when the Holy Spirit prays in us." When there is yieldedness to Him, when there is obedience to Him, when there is faith in God, when we are praying in the will of God—that's praying in the Spirit of God. And I think of our Lord's words in Luke 18:1 that men "ought always to pray, and not to faint." Let me go back to Dr. Torrey and leave this first weapon with a comment from him: "Prayer brings the power of God into our work." And I say, "Amen." We cannot have too much prayer, but, alas and alack, too frequently we have too little.

There is a second weapon that God has put at our disposal—the power of godly living. "Ye are the salt of the earth," said the Lord Jesus. A scene comes to my mind that is related in Genesis 18. Three men traveling in the Holy Land were approaching the city of Hebron. They came to the plains of Mamre where Abraham had set up his tent, and an incident occurred there after Abraham had fed them. Before they left, they said, "Shall we not share with Abraham the thing which God is about to do?" And they evidently told him of the impending destruction of Sodom and Gomorrah.

Abraham undoubtedly thought of Lot and his family and began to speak to God. You know the story. "Peradventure there are fifty righteous within the city: wilt thou consume and not spare the place?" (v. 24). And God answered, "If I find . . . fifty righteous . . . I will spare all the place for their sake" (v. 26). Fifty righteous souls would have meant deliverance from the judgment of God about to fall on that wicked city. But that's not the end, for Abraham kept up his plea, and he went from fifty to forty. And from forty to thirty. And from thirty to twenty. And from twenty to ten. And God said, "I will not destroy it for the ten's sake" (v. 32).

Do you see that this passage is telling us that in the economy and government of God, He will withhold judgment if there are those who are righteous within the place where judgment is to be poured out. Do you see that if there had been ten righteous souls in Sodom and Gomorrah, they would have meant more to those cities than all their standing armies and all the acumen and strategy of their generals. And it is my judgment that holy men and holy women who know and love God, whose names have never sounded in the halls of any congress, or any parliament, have done more to sustain nations than the armies thereof.

But there may come a day when even the righteous in a land will not hold back that land from judgment. Listen to this. This is an overpowering word. "Son of man, when a land sinneth against me by committing a trespass, and I stretch out my hand upon it, and break the staff of the bread thereof, and send famine upon it, and cut off from it man and beast; though these three men, Noah, Daniel, and Job, were in it, they should deliver but their own souls by their righteousness, saith the Lord Jehovah" (Eze 14:13-14). And look at verse 20: "Though Noah, Daniel, and Job, were in it, as I live, saith the Lord Jehovah, they should deliver neither son nor daughter; they should but deliver their own souls by their righteousness."

There will come the day, and one wonders whether it may not be coming very soon, for the nations of the earth today, when judgment will fall. Certainly when the Lord comes for His own, and those who know and love the Lord are caught up together in clouds to meet Him in the air, the time of dire and awful judgment will begin. But until that day, when in the purposes of God it is God's action to bring judgment without remedy, the righteous are the salt of the earth. This is a weapon. It's a great weapon. It's a weapon that speaks to the hearts of sinners. It's a weapon that brings a sense of the presence of God and gives courage to the Christian. "Ye are the salt of the earth." McCheyne wrote: "A holy minister is an awful weapon in the hand of God."

Weapon number three is the power of faith. For, says the Word of God, "without faith it is impossible to be well-pleasing unto him." We stand in a terrifying day. But that is no reason to be discouraged. That is no reason to seek out some place where we may hide ourselves and await the coming holocaust. Let us dare to believe God. Listen to these verses from which God has been speaking to me. James 1:6-8: "Let him ask in faith, nothing doubting: . . . let not that man think that he shall receive anything of the Lord; a doubleminded man, unstable in all his ways." Mark 9:23: "All things are possible to him that believeth." And Mark 11:22: "Have faith in God." That last text was paraphrased by Hudson Taylor: "Hold God's faithfulness."

Whatever the earthly scene, you and I can, in absolute trust in God, go forward. Let us dare to believe God—that God will yet honor His word; that God will yet vindicate His saints; that God will yet, according to His program, bring in the universal reign of righteousness and truth when His Son comes again. So, thank God, we can believe God. And I really think that the harder it is to believe, the better God likes it, and the greater He will reward it. So, let's dare to hold onto our faithful God.

The fourth weapon is the power of truth. Said the Lord Jesus in His high-priestly prayer, "Thy word is truth." Let's think of this for a moment. What was it the Lord Jesus had said? You'll find it in John 8:32: "Ye shall know the truth, and the truth shall make you free." Truth has power to deliver from error—from error about God and self and Satan and the hereafter. Truth also has power to deliver from the dominion of sin. There is a self-contained power in the truth of God that vibrates with delivering life. That's one of the reasons we should hide it in our hearts. It not only is good advice; it's great power. Isn't that a striking word Paul uses in 2 Corinthians 13:8: "We can do nothing against the truth, but for the truth." And that's true. In an ultimate sense, when all is done, when all is finished, when the whole course is wound up, truth is going to emerge victorious. And nothing and no one can hold it back. The Word of God will be vindicated.

Frankly, I don't think it takes any ingenuity for a simplehearted child of God, reading the Word of God, to see that the truth of God as to the course of this age is moving on just as God said it would. I remember my teachers years ago saying that the very infidels in the pulpits were a proof of the accuracy and the truth of God's Word, because God's Word said that in the last days they would arise, speaking evil things. And so I say to my dear Christian friends, The train's on time, the schedule's right, and we're moving inexorably to the final triumph. The weapon of the power of prayer, the weapon of the power of godly living, the weapon of faith, the weapon of truth.

Let me mention the weapon of the power of love. Galatians 5:6 speaks of "faith working through love." Oh, the power of love. "Now abideth faith, hope, love, these three; and the greatest of these is love" (1 Co 13:13). Because of the bitterness of the adversary, because of the cruelty of the circumstances through which you have to move, has your heart shriveled up in malice and bitterness and hatred? Where is the love among us? I am not speaking of condoning sin. Not for one moment would I crown unbelief as worthy. But I still believe it's possible to love men who are actually their own greatest enemies. And so the Word of God reads, "If a man say, I love God, and hateth his brother, he is a liar" (1 Jn 4:20). Now that's as direct preaching as I think I've ever heard. And the verse goes on: "He that loveth not his brother whom he hath seen, cannot love God whom he hath not seen." Oh, that we would know that presence of the Spirit of God in such a heart-warming manner that, despite some differences—not the difference of unbelief and belief but the differences between those who are truly God's children—we might be overcome in love. I know of nothing that is more calculated to be a weapon in our hands than to love our foes. "Love your enemies, do good to them that hate you" (Lk 6:27). May God give us to know how to love.

But there's a final word—the power of hope. This is a great weapon God has given us. For hope isn't a weak, namby-pamby word. Its true meaning is not reflected in the way it has come to be used in the twentieth century. It's a strong word. It means something that I expect with my whole heart. And not only do I expect it, it's what I desire above everything else. Hope! And God has given us hope. "Now the God of hope fill you with all joy and peace in believing, that ye may abound in hope, in the power of the Holy Spirit" (Ro 15:13). And so there is hope for us.

You ask, "With all that's going on in the world, how can you be hopeful?" And I answer you, as a child of God, having the Word of God, How can I be hopeless?" Hope-full, we should be. For you see, we have God's present protection. And not only so, we have both God's present control and His future reign. For 1 Corinthians 15:25 says, "He must reign."

So, very simply, God has given us some weapons which are not carnal, but which are mighty, which are able to pull down strongholds. And I believe that as you and I mean business with God and lay hold of prayer and consecration and faith and truth and love and hope, we'll begin to wield the weapons that will count for God. The weapons of our warfare are not carnal, but are mighty, to the casting down of strongholds. Let us use them by the power of the Spirit.

1969

The Sanctions of God

> When thy judgments are in the earth, the inhabitants of the world learn righteousness (Is 26:9).
> Thy judgments are a great deep: O Jehovah (Ps 36:6).
> For Jehovah will rise up as in mount Perazim, he will be wroth as in the valley of Gibeon; that he may do his work, his strange work, and bring to pass his act, his strange act. Now therefore be ye not scoffers, lest your bonds be made strong; for a decree of destruction have I heard from the Lord, Jehovah of hosts, upon the whole earth (Is 28:21-22).

THOUGH IT IS DENIED by some and carelessly forgotten by others, God is a God of government, of judgment, of justice. Bless His name, He is also the God of all grace (1 Pe 5:10). This significant word is given of our Lord in John 1:14, that He is "full of grace and truth." May I observe that that is the proper combination. Grace without truth is license; truth without grace is hopelessness. But it is not *some* grace and *some* truth, so that the result is neither. It is not a hybrid of grace and truth. It is perfect and undiluted grace and perfect and undiluted truth—neither one diminished by the other. He is full of grace and truth. Such is the perfection of our God.

Because of the burden of my heart, I want to address myself now to the matter of God's government, though, of course, I caution you not to forget His grace. I have in mind just one area of divine revelation: the sanctions of God. By this term "sanctions," I have two matters in view. First, that violation of God's laws necessarily involves punishment. Second, that God has set up principles, considerations, influences to impel men to moral action.

Of the former—that violation of God's law necessarily involves punishment—it may be said that God has His laws and they are not broken with impunity. A writer in one of the daily papers last Saturday wrote that certain recent events "symbolize the collapse of conventional ethics. Commandments are no longer written in stone." But may I counter? No one breaks the laws of God. Rather the transgressor sooner or later is broken by God's law. You see, when we sin we set up processes of action which will take their toll in this life and in the next, unless an atonement is found. Nor do we affect only ourselves when we sin; present and future generations are involved. I cannot too strongly affirm that the teaching of the Word of God is that sin has in itself the seeds of destruction for the perpetrator thereof. There is a price that is paid. There are wages of sin.

The Word of God reads, "Jehovah, Jehovah, a God merciful and gracious, slow to anger, and abundant in lovingkindness and truth; keeping lovingkindness for thousands, forgiving iniquity and transgression and sin; and that will by no means clear the guilty, visiting the iniquity of the fathers upon the children, and upon the children's children, upon the third and upon the fourth generation" (Ex 34:6-7). The context makes clear that Moses wanted to know the ways of God. God said He would show him His glory and make all His goodness pass before him. I believe the verses that I have just read give in epitome that revelation of the ways of God, the glory of God and the goodness of God. It goes in two directions —mercy to the repentant, judgment to the unrepentant. This is part of the very nature of God. And, indeed, God has seen to it that sin carries its own seeds of destruction within itself.

It seems to me that the text for our generation is "Be not deceived; God is not mocked: for whatsoever a man soweth, that shall he also reap" (Gal 6:7). Or, in the words of James, equally relevant: "When lust hath conceived, it bringeth forth sin: and sin, when it is finished, bringeth forth death" (Ja 1:15, KJV). I remember hearing a preacher years ago ring the changes on that little clause, "when it is finished." "When it is *finished.*" "Sin, when it is *finished.*" I remember his rhetorical question, "When is it finished?" and his conclusion, "It is never finished!" For anarchy against God —rebellion against the laws of God—carries in itself the seeds of its destruction of the sinner. If there were not a hopeful word of the gospel, we would all be undone.

What I am affirming with regard to the judgment of sin is not to deny that a sinner can find forgiveness. No one needs despair of forgiveness if he turns to God with repentance toward God and faith toward our Lord Jesus Christ. But neither do I want to give the impression that sin does not matter. And to take a step further, I don't want to give the impression that even sin that is forgiven does not matter. Forces are released when we sin that go on and on. And while we may be forgiven by the grace of God, that is not to say that these forces shall be altogether stayed. There are consequences of even forgiven sin.

Forces of evil in themselves—or as an example—set up that which must necessarily follow as their natural course. Sin carries its own seeds of destruction. Manasseh was the king of Judah. He was an evil king, but God permitted something to come into his life that brought him to repentance and contrition. And the Scripture asserts that he knew God. He was followed by another wicked king by the name of Amon who was followed by another king that normally we think of as good in at least a limited sense—Josiah. God had indicated that judgment was going to fall upon Judah because of the sins of Manasseh, and even though Manasseh repented afterward and even though there was a revival under Josiah afterward, God still said, "Judah shall go into captivity because of the sin of Manasseh." The results of Manasseh's sin still took their toll, even though he repented and even though a revival came before the judgment fell. I think it's important, if we see nothing else, that we see this. So turn to 2 Chronicles 33:

> And Jehovah spake to Manasseh, and to his people; but they gave no heed. Wherefore Jehovah brought upon them the captains of the host of the king of Assyria, who took Manasseh in chains, and bound him with fetters, and carried him to Babylon. And when he was in distress, he besought Jehovah his God, and humbled himself greatly before the God of his fathers. And he prayed unto him; and he was entreated of him, and heard his supplication, and brought him again to Jerusalem into his kingdom. Then Manasseh knew that Jehovah he was God (vv. 10-13).

Notice it says he "humbled himself greatly before the God of his fathers." So you say, "Yes, he sinned; he was an evil king. But

THE SANCTIONS OF GOD 165

he repented." Thank God he repented. But I want you to see something else: His son Amon followed in the first steps of his father. But Josiah came to the throne, and let me read just two verses about Josiah. God is speaking to Josiah:

> Because thy heart was tender, and thou didst humble thyself before Jehovah, when thou heardest what I spake against this place, and against the inhabitants thereof, that they should become a desolation and a curse, and hast rent thy clothes, and wept before me; I also have heard thee, saith Jehovah. Therefore, behold, I will gather thee to thy fathers, and thou shalt be gathered to thy grave in peace, neither shall thine eyes see all the evil which I will bring upon this place (2 Ki 22:19-20).

Yes, Josiah repaired the temple. The book of the law was found as they cleansed the temple. Josiah instituted great reforms. "Surely then," you say, "the wickedness of Manasseh having been pardoned by God and the good works of Josiah having occurred, God will not punish His people." But look at this:

> Notwithstanding, Jehovah turned not from the fierceness of his great wrath, wherewith his anger was kindled against Judah, because of all the provocations wherewith Manasseh had provoked him. And Jehovah said, I will remove Judah also out of my sight, as I have removed Israel, and I will cast off this city which I have chosen, even Jerusalem, and the house of which I said, My name shall be there (2 Ki 23:26-27).

There you are. A man who dishonored God, who lived a life of a profligate in insurrection against the laws of God—even though he came to a better mind and even though he was followed by a grandson whom we could call good—the evil influences of Manasseh's life kept on. And "judgment was to fall because of Manasseh."

What shall I say about the tragic story of David and Bathsheba? Was David forgiven? This is his confession: "I acknowledged my sin unto thee, and mine iniquity did I not hide: I said, I will confess my transgressions unto Jehovah; and thou forgavest the iniquity of my sin" (Ps 32:5). But the sin he had committed set up processes in life which continued, which even the forgiveness of God did not stay. The child born out of wedlock to Bathsheba and to

David died. And the effects of David's sin were reflected in his children (2 Sa 12:9-11). Would David commit adultery? Then his son Ammon would follow his example and outrage his half sister. Would David have Uriah put in the thick of the battle so that he would be killed? Then Absalom, David's son, would follow his example and kill his half brother Ammon. Would David rebel against God? Then David would know the rebellion of Absalom against himself. The whole sordid story follows in the train of David's terrible sin.

The truth involved here may not stop us in our headlong flight into sin. But it ought to make us stop and think. Sin has its own consequences.

It's this very truth—that sin carries with it its own destruction—which frightens me concerning our own nation and our world today. Many of our young people—thinking they are free—are plunging into sin, believing there is pleasure therein. But, oh, what a rude awakening is ahead. Preachers and teachers long since turning from the Word of God encourage the permissiveness of the day—indeed, even counsel the flouting of the laws of God. These preachers and teachers will some day be set upon as the cause of the suffering, the shame, the disillusionment of these same young people in days to come. There's a price to be paid for sin.

God is a God of government and there are the sanctions of God. But let me turn to the teachings of the Word of God that impinge on this matter of doctrine which should impel to moral action. There is not only the natural truth that sin curses and brings forth death; there is also the revelation of the sanctions of God as part of His direct attempt to bring us to His will.

Now there is a mystery about God's sanctions. I think that is what the psalmist had in mind in Psalm 36:6, with which we began: "Thy judgments are a great deep: O Jehovah." Mysterious, deep, unfathomable are the ways of God. The psalmist said elsewhere: "Thy way was in the sea, and thy paths in the great waters, and thy footsteps were not known" (Ps 77:19). And nowhere are the ways of God more difficult to follow than in the execution of His judgments in the earth. The problem of the suffering of the righteous and the seeming prosperity of the wicked concerns a whole book of the Bible—the book of Job—to say nothing of Psalms 37 and 73.

I think there are some things that, as we proceed, we must keep in mind, perhaps as a warning, lest we come to erroneous conclusions. First, do not make the mistake of Eliphaz and Bildad and Zophar in the book of Job and conclude that all suffering is because of personal acts of transgression. Some suffering undoubtedly is, but not all. The purposes of God in allowing trial and suffering are manifold: for the cultivation of our holiness; for the strengthening of others when they are tested; for the directing of men's minds to God as the only one who could enable them to triumph in severe testing; for the purpose of glory of God now and hereafter. Let us be careful not to point the finger and say, as the friends of Job did, "It's because you're so great a sinner." There's a mystery in the dealings of God, and we do not always know the answer.

The second warning, I think, is that even when God acts to judge men, no one dares conclude that such a judgment brands those judged as sinners beyond the rest of men. Listen to the Word of God:

> Now there were some present at that very season who told him of the Galileans, whose blood Pilate had mingled with their sacrifices. And he answered and said unto them, Think ye that these Galileans were sinners above all the Galileans, because they have suffered these things? I tell you, Nay: but, except ye repent, ye shall all in like manner perish. Or those eighteen, upon whom the tower in Siloam fell, and killed them, think ye that they were offenders above all the men that dwell in Jerusalem? I tell you, Nay: but, except ye repent, ye shall all likewise perish (Lk 13:1-5).

Another warning that I think we must bear in mind is that while "some men's sins are evident, going before unto judgment," it is said of other men that "they follow after" (1 Ti 5:24). So there are judgments which are present and discernible and there are judgments which follow after. One of the reasons involved in the mystery of the execution of God's sanctions is that God does not always act quickly; and because God's judgment is delayed, men sometimes come to the conclusion it is denied. That is not true. Let's be careful about that. I think this fact is forgotten both by the saint and the sinner. The psalmist was an example of this. After describing the apparent lack of judgment in the life of the ungodly and after decrying his own suffering, he says: "When I thought how I might know this, it was too painful for me; until I went into the sanctuary of God, and considered their latter end" (Ps 73:16-17). As Dr. Robert G. Lee so often used to tell us, "Payday—Someday." Maybe not today, but someday. The ungodly man, smug in his luxury and content in seeming to get away with his perfidy, presumes upon the grace of God, only in the end to face the judgment of God.

There's a fourth observation that I'd like to make: that the mystery of God's sanctions is further deepened by God's great desire to show mercy. Isaiah's word is applicable here: destruction from His hand, the mighty overwhelming judgments of the Most High, are (to use Isaiah's words) His strange work. I think all of us should be heartened by that message; for if we received from the hand of the Lord that which we really deserve, each one of us would have perished long ago. That the long-suffering of God should lead sinners to repentance is the purpose of God's patience, according to Romans 2:4. But I remind you that grace rejected serves only to underline the justice of the penalty (Ro 2:5). Remember, too, that it is as true today as in Noah's day that God's Spirit will not always strive with man.

There is not only the mystery of God's sanctions, there is also the revelation of the manifestations of God's sanctions and these are warnings God sets up and speaks to in His Word. There are times when God acts, and these are sobering flashes of what must face men who play fast and loose with His laws.

I want to speak both to saints and sinners here. What are these principles, these considerations, these influences which impel to moral action, which God has set before us in His Word? For His saint they are—in part: First, He allows trials, testing of one sort or another, to come. When we take the law into our own hands, when willfully we turn from the known will of God and persist and insist on our own wills, because He's a loving heavenly Father, He will chastise us. Certain passages in the Scripture are classics in the development of this theme. One of them is in Hebrews 12, which reads in part: "Ye have not yet resisted unto blood, striving

THE SANCTIONS OF GOD 169

against sin: and ye have forgotten the exhortation which reasoneth with you as with sons, My son, regard not lightly the chastening of the Lord, nor faint when thou art reproved of him" (vv. 4-5). They had not "resisted unto blood, striving against sin." What is this saying? It is saying that sin had the mastery over them; they didn't resist. In the power of the Spirit of God, they didn't take their stand; and when sin came in like a flood, it overwhelmed them. You've heard me say it before: God doesn't want spoiled children. He reproves, and testing comes.

There were those in Corinth who in an unworthy manner were partaking of the Lord's Supper. When the believers gathered together for the *agape,* the love feast, these disorderly ones gluttonously devoured the food, and when it was time to partake of the Lord's Supper, they were in a stupor, they were drunken, and they were partaking of the Lord's Supper in an unworthy manner. "For this cause," says Paul, "many among you are weak and sickly" (1 Co 11:30). God was judging. God was reproving.

Testing is one way in which God impels us to moral action in accordance with His will. But that's not all. There is a second thing—death. Did you know that if you persist in your disobedience, God may even take you home rather than let your soul be lost? This is a sobering word. These are the sanctions of God. Read 1 Corinthians 11:30 again: "For this cause many among you are weak and sickly, and not a few sleep." You know what that means: Not a few of you have died. "But if we discerned ourselves [if we judged ourselves], we should not be judged. But when we are judged, we are chastened of the Lord, that we may not be condemned with the world" (vv. 31-32). It is not up to you and me to point our fingers at anyone and say he's an example of this. But here is a pertinent word of sobering warning to you and to me personally. The first and second sanctions of God are trials and death.

The third evidence of the sanctions of God is in your conscience. I have been amazed, as I have thumbed through the pages of the New Testament, to see the tremendous emphasis on conscience in the Word of God. Outstanding among all the characters in the New Testament who made much of this matter of a good conscience was Paul (see Ac 23:1; 24:16; 2 Co 1:12; 1 Ti 1:5). I don't hear much about conscience anymore. But the Word of God has a lot to say about it. I'm going to give you just one verse because it spoke so deeply to my own heart, and I needed the word. In 1 Timothy 1:5 Paul wrote, "The end of the charge [the object of the charge, the goal that is before you and the charge I'm making to you] is love out of a pure heart and a good conscience and faith unfeigned." Three things, and one of these is a good conscience. Oh, that we would know a good conscience. Not simply because in penitence we have come to the Lord for forgiveness (Thank God that is open to us; we can have our conscience cleansed from dead works, in order to serve the living God), but because in the power of the Spirit of God we have walked in obedience and our conscience does not accuse us.

The fourth sanction for the believer is the coming of the Lord and the subsequent dissolution of the heavens and the earth as they now are. The text, which I think most of you know, that has spoken so deeply to my own heart in this regard is 1 John 2:28: "My little children, abide in him; that, if he shall be manifested, we may . . . not be ashamed before him at his coming." I wish I could share with you something of the sense of awe in my own soul in the light of that text. Those of you who can read it in the original, do so. Those of you who can't, look at the margin of the American Standard Version. It's to "be ashamed from before him at his coming." I don't know all that means and I don't want to know what it means in experience. The Lord Jesus says, "I'm coming again. How will you meet Me?"

And the fifth sanction of God is the judgment seat of Christ. "So then each one of us shall give account of himself to God" (Ro 14:12). "We must all be made manifest before the judgment-seat of Christ; that each one may receive the things done in the body, according to what he hath done, whether it be good or bad" (2 Co 5:10). That's real, my brother, my sister. It's going to happen. And may God make it plain to my own heart, as under God I try to make it plain to your hearts.

These are God's principles, God's considerations, God's influences that impel us to moral action.

What I have said concerning the saint has its parallel in the teaching of Scripture concerning the sinner. First, God may send trial to the sinner in an attempt to bring him to a better mind. Pharaoh, in the obstinancy and stubbornness of his heart, refused to repent (Ex 9:6-7). But Nebuchadnezzar, with his hair long and his fingernails long, and his body wet with the dew of heaven, at last came to contrition and confessed: "I . . . praise and extol and honor the King of heaven" (Dan 4:37). God attempts by testing to bring sinners to a recognition of their need of Himself.

Second, sometimes, strangely enough—and here is the evidence of the mystery of God's dealings—He attempts to do it by kindness and patience. In Romans 2:4-5 the apostle is saying that God, by His goodness, is attempting to bring man to repentance. "Despisest thou the riches of his goodness and forbearance and longsuffering, not knowing that the goodness of God leadeth thee to repentance?" (v. 4). That's God's purpose. But if God's goodness is taken advantage of, then this is true: "After thy hardness and impenitent heart [thou] treasurest up for thyself wrath in the day of wrath and revelation of the righteous judgment of God" (v. 5).

Third, in the same chapter there is a word about the conscience of the unsaved man: ". . . that they show the work of the law written in their hearts, their conscience bearing witness therewith, and their thoughts one with another accusing or else excusing them; in the day when God shall judge the secrets of men according to my gospel, by Jesus Christ" (vv. 15-16).

There's a fourth thing I just must bring in: God has seen to it that there is a dissatisfaction of soul, an emptiness of life for the worldling, unless the worldling comes to God, who alone can satisfy. Thank God for that longing of soul, that dissatisfaction, that understanding that life must be more than the sinner has been able to find in it. That's what Ecclesiastes is all about—the monotony of life, the dissatisfactions of soul with all that is under the sun—until you have that exhortation: "Remember also thy Creator in the days of thy youth, before the evil days come, and the years draw nigh, when thou shalt say, I have no pleasure in them" (Ec 12:1).

Then there is a fifth great sanction God has mentioned in His Word. It has to do with eternity, with the judgment and the wrath to come. It has to do with the place of which the Lord Jesus said, "There shall be the weeping and the gnashing of teeth" (Mt

13:42). And the plea of John the Baptist was: "Flee from the wrath to come" (Mt 3:7).

I have dealt only with the sanctions of God concerning individuals. There are also His sanctions which involve institutions. Don't think I haven't thought about that, because Moody Bible Institute is an institution. There are His sanctions which have to do with nations. And the rise or fall of nations is not apart from the judgments of God which are in the earth.

However, all of these sanctions may not be enough. Somehow the perfidy of the human heart is such that even when we know better we sin. What can I say? Well, these things I have said should sober us. They should make us stop and think.

But I think there's one matter left. God has erected a supreme barrier on the road to judgment. Listen to hymn writer, James Montgomery:

> With forbidden pleasures would this vain world charm,
> All its sordid treasures spread to work me harm.
> Bring to my remembrance sad Gethsemane,
> Or, in darker semblance, cross-crowned Calvary.

Remember the Saviour who died *on Calvary*. And if this doesn't arrest us, if this doesn't stop us in our mad plunge to the judgment that sin executes, then there is no hope. The six hours of excruciating pain, of unbearable agony, of incalculable suffering, when He bore in His own body our sins to the tree—these are our trenchant witnesses to the heinousness of sin. When there was no other way, when salvation could be found by no other expedient, God was willing to let His Son pay the penalty of our sins. So I take you to Calvary, and every stripe upon His back, and every bruise upon His face, and every thorn prick upon His brow, and every nail wound in His hands and side, and every taunt and curse He bore, and every indignity He suffered at the moment He dismissed His spirit—all cry out, "Sin is a terrible thing, sin is a hateful thing, sin is an awful thing." So my appeal to you is to forsake evilness and to do good, to abhor sin, to turn to the Lord while He may be found, while He is near. The old hymn writer was right:

> Hasten, sinners, to be wise.
> Stay not for tomorrow's sun.
> Wisdom if thou still despise,
> Harder is it to be won.

Is God saying anything to you? Is the Spirit of God putting His finger on anything in your life? Is God saying, "Son, daughter, judgment is my strange work, my strange act. But I do reprove, I do judge." Stop. In love turn from your sin to the Saviour.

1970
Our Mainstay in the Evil Hour

THERE ARE MANY demanding subjects and themes that may be well spoken to from the Word of God in an hour like this. Frankly, it was difficult to make a choice among them. However, I have sensed the leading of the Lord to address myself, I hope in a new and informative way, to a most basic subject, a subject which has eternal significance, a subject which will continue as our interest and concern and our reason for thanksgiving to God long after current problems have ceased to be. I want to speak about the blood of Christ. That blood speaks to our ills and our plight today.

Surely no Bible-taught Christian can doubt that the enemy has come in like a flood in this twentieth century. Blatant godlessness, unashamed immodesty and immorality, crass materialism, worldly pleasure, self-seeking, apostasy in the visible church, injustice, revolt against God are on every hand. Let me, therefore, speak to this theme: "Our Mainstay in the Evil Hour, the Blood of Christ."

There are other defenses in an hour like this. Obedience to the Word of God; earnest, importunate, intercessory prayer; fellowship of believers; fullness of the Holy Spirit; faith and hope; but I turn to just one issue—the blood of Christ. Despised by some, denied by others, relegated to antiquity by the so-called learned, it is the very crux of the matter for all of life to the Bible believer.

The blood of Christ was shed for many unto the remission of sins (Mt 26:28). It was God's own blood with which He purchased the church (Ac 20:28). We have been redeemed by the blood (Eph 1:7). By the blood we have been brought near (Eph 2:13). It is the blood of sprinkling (1 Pe 1:2). It is the precious blood (1 Pe 1:19). It is the blood of the cross whereby He has made peace (Col 1:20). It has cleansed our consciences from dead works so that we can serve the living God (Heb 9:14). By it we have been saved and washed (1 Jn 1:7), and by it we have been loosed from our sins (Rev 1:5). In it we have washed our robes and made them white (Rev 7:14). By it we have boldness to enter into the holy place (Heb 10:19). By it we are sanctified (Heb 13:12). By it we conquer the devil (Rev 12:11). It is the blood of the eternal covenant that binds us to God forever (Heb 13:20). Is it any wonder, therefore, that early proclaimers of the gospel of Christ used as their motto and their maxim, "Sanguis Christi, Christi evangelium"—the blood of Christ is the gospel of Christ. It is the basic truth of our relationship to God.

Why blood? Why was the shedding of blood necessary? There are some interesting passages in the Book of God on this theme, and I want to turn to a few of them. Blood was not to be eaten, and there are two passages in particular that cite this.

In Genesis 9:4-5 we read: "But flesh with the life thereof, which is the blood thereof, shall ye not eat. And surely your blood, the blood of your lives, will I require . . . and at the hand of man, even at the hand of every man's brother, will I require the life of man." In verse 4, two matters are put in apposition, one over against the other. It says, "flesh with the life thereof, which is the blood thereof." The words "life" and "blood" in Genesis 9:4 are in apposition as indicating that they present a single truth from a slightly different viewpoint. The life is the blood; the blood is the life.

Having said that, very interestingly the word translated "life" in Genesis 9:4 is translated many times elsewhere in the Old Testament as "soul." I am not insisting that it be so translated here, except that I think that at once we are face to face with a great mystery. There is some inner meaning, there is some inner life that is associated with the blood, and to bring that out forcibly, let me translate it this way: "But flesh with the soul thereof, which is the blood thereof." I recognize that the word for "soul" is translated in different ways in the Old Testament and it has different meanings. Its original meaning is that which breathes, but then it comes to stand for the inner life of a living being. We speak of the soul. I am not saying that the soul is in the blood, but it is certainly represented by the blood at the very least. There is a deeper significance than just the physical fluid of the blood according to this passage in the Word of God. The word "soul" or "life" is associated with the word "blood," and it is for that reason that the blood was not to be eaten, according to the teaching of Genesis 9.

The second passage is similar. In Deuteronomy 12:23 we read: "Only be sure that thou eat not the blood: for the blood is the life; and thou shalt not eat the life with the flesh." Notice once again the little word "life." It is the word that I have already spoken to in Genesis 9:4. It is the word "soul." And again, while I am not insisting that it has to be so translated here, I am endeavoring to put across the idea that there is a sacredness, an inner meaning, a soulish significance of some kind attached to the blood. Let me read it in that way: "Only be sure that thou eat not the blood: for the blood is the soul."

Now we are ready to turn to a third passage of Scripture. We have indicated the sacredness of the blood as associated with the inner life of the man. The third passage of Scripture will show why that blood, sacred in its significance, is associated with atonement. The passage is Leviticus 17:11: "For the life of the flesh is in the blood; and I have given it to you upon the altar to make atonement for your souls: for it is the blood that maketh atonement by reason of the life." If you have a marginal reference Bible, perchance you will see the very thing of which I have been speaking—that the word "life" in Leviticus 17:11 is the word "soul." It is so designated in the margin of the American Standard Version, for example. Now let me read it that way: "For the soul of the flesh is in the blood; and I have given it to you upon the altar to make atonement for your souls: for it is the blood that maketh atonement by reason of the soul."

That is the reason God chose blood—because of the sacredness, this association with the inner life of man, this soulish significance whatever it is. I admit I am beyond my depth, but it has taught me at least this much: to see the sacred, holy relationship of blood to man's life, man's soul. That is the reason God chose blood.

Before I go on, let me point out this. Nowhere in the Old Testament, so far as I have been able to ascertain, is the word "spirit" associated with "blood." It is always "soul," never "spirit." Now our Lord died, but of His death (I want you right at the outset to see the superlative nature of the death which He died) it is recorded: "For if the blood of goats and bulls, and the ashes of a heifer sprinkling them that have been defiled, sanctify unto the cleanness of the flesh: how much more shall the blood of Christ, who through the eternal Spirit offered himself without blemish unto God, cleanse your conscience from dead works to serve the living God?" (Heb 9:13-14).

Here is the supremacy of our Lord's sacrifice that goes beyond anything that an Old Testament sacrifice could do for the offerer. Notice it again: "If the blood of goats and bulls, and the ashes of a heifer . . . sanctify unto the cleanness of the flesh: how much more shall the blood of Chris*t who through the eternal Spirit, offered himself without blemish,"* how much more shall that blood "cleanse your conscience from dead works to serve the living God?" Our Lord's offering involved His whole being. As the Son of God and the Son of man He gave Himself for us—body, soul and spirit.

Having said that much, how significant becomes the word that John the Baptist spoke when our Lord came to the Jordan to be baptized: "Behold, the Lamb of God" (Jn 1:29, 36). I am told that according to the custom in the tradition of the fathers, when the Passover time came in antiquity, the father of the house would select the lamb, the lamb which met the requirements prescribed in the Word of God; and that lamb was designated as *God's lamb.* It was dedicated to God. It was set apart for the use which God had prescribed for it—the slaying of it, the eating of the flesh, the reminder of God's deliverance in Egypt. All of these things were involved in the selection of that lamb. It was God's lamb. But after the passing of centuries, ultimately there came one who was not simply a lamb of God, but as John announced, "Behold, *the* Lamb of God." All other lambs were insignificant alongside this Lamb. Here truly is God's Lamb. He came to shed His blood, His holy blood, His sacred blood.

Moreover, you've noticed, haven't you, in the Old Testament how that on occasion an adjective is used for blood, an adjective which indicates morality; so it is innocent blood (Ps 94:21; 106:38; Pr 6:17, etc), it is righteous blood (Mt 23:35). There is some kind of unity of the soul and blood thus taught in these scriptures at which we have looked.

Now I am ready to launch into three thoughts from the Word of God which are a great mainstay to me in my need of the blood of

Christ. First of all may I suggest that the blood of the Lord Jesus is necessary to salvation. It is the basis of salvation. All I need to do is read some scriptures and remind you of this truth. Listen to 1 Peter 1:18-19: "Knowing that ye were redeemed, not with corruptible things, with silver or gold, from your vain manner of life handed down from your fathers; but with precious blood, as of a lamb without blemish and without spot, even the blood of Christ."

Ah, how basic this is. I know it is refused by many. I know that individuals wise beyond their own conceits spurn the doctrine of the shed blood of the Lord Jesus. But whatever men may say, the Word of God makes much of the blood of Christ. We've been bought with that blood. Salvation is dependent upon the shedding of that blood, for I remind you that without the shedding of blood there is no remission (Heb 9:22). So, dear friend, let's remember the blood that was shed. Remember the language of the song writer:

> He to rescue me from danger,
> Interposed His precious blood.

You say, "We know this. We've known it for years." I say to you, "Praise God if you have, but is there not in your heart some praise to God this morning, some recognition perhaps in a new way of the wonder of it all?" He loved me and gave Himself for me!

A number of years ago when I was a pastor in the East I was called upon to go on conference ministry very frequently. And as the Lord enabled me and I could absent myself from the local church of which I was the pastor, I did so. I remember one summer I received an invitation to go to a nearby city. It was the kind of conference in which the local people came in from their own homes rather than going to a conference grounds where room and board were provided. I was able to get away, so I accepted two evening engagements. As I went I felt very much at a loss. Normally a speaker in a conference knows something of the spirit of the conference and then he can fit in. In this instance I was going in cold. I remember thinking, *The Lord is certainly going to have to help me in an unusual way here.* As I went into the church, as I recall, the leader of the conference came and greeted me. I thought, *This is my opportunity.* I suppose I should have learned to depend on the Lord without asking human help. At any rate, I said to him, "How are the meetings going?" I thought his answer would give me a clue as to whether I was on the right track with what I had on my mind to speak about. He answered, "Oh, they've been going very well." Well, I was insistent, and so I said, "What about . . ." and I named the man who had preached the night before, a man I knew very well. "How was he, and what happened?" "Oh, you know him," he said. "He just preaches the gospel."

Well, I did something that night I don't often do, but I might as well confess that I did it. I got talking about the cross, and I said something like this, "Has the cross and its meaning grown dim to you? Can you think about the cross without shedding tears? Has the whole thing become so commonplace to you, so everydayish, that you're not moved anymore? Sure, let's grant that the doctrines connected with the cross, at least the doctrines most of us know, are the milk of the Word rather than the meat of the Word. Let's grant that, but has your taste grown less for a good cold drink once in a while? Have you spent enough time at the foot of the cross to say with wonder, 'He loved me and gave Himself for me?' " I tried to point out we are in serious spiritual difficulty when the cross loses its wonder to our souls. I'll say for the man, he came to me afterward and said, "I deserved it."

Ah, my friends, the blood of Christ is precious blood. Let's stay at the foot of the cross awhile. What does it say? We were redeemed, we were bought with precious blood as of a lamb without blemish and without spot, even the blood of Christ. I am here to say I know of no other ground on which to stand, in time or eternity, than this ground. He shed His precious blood for my sins.

But that's not the only passage. There are many others. Let me turn to just one other, Romans 3:24-26, starting with the last two words of verse 24: ". . . Christ Jesus: whom God set forth to be a propitiation, through faith, in his blood, to show his righteousness because of the passing over of the sins done aforetime, in the forbearance of God; for the showing, I say, of his righteousness at this present season: that he might himself be just, and the justifier of him that hath faith in Jesus." Here is a passage of Scripture which, to me, beyond any other shows to me the answer to the insoluble problem to men, of how sinful men may be accepted by a holy God.

Men seek to answer that question by saying there is no sin, and therefore there is no problem. Or by saying sin isn't so bad, and therefore God will forgive us freely and lightly without any satisfaction being made. That is not God's answer. Did you see twice over in these verses that God's righteousness is involved in what the Lord Jesus did, so that He could be just and the Justifier of Him that believeth in Jesus. Calvary is not just an excess bit of impedimenta so far as God is concerned. It is the absolute essential and the unequivocable demand of God if men are ever to be forgiven.

We live in a light age indeed, an age in which God is sort of a grandfather; anybody does anything he wants to do to Him and it doesn't matter. That's not my understanding of the Bible teaching about God. "It is a fearful thing to fall into the hands of the living God" (Heb 10:31). "Our God is a consuming fire" (Heb 12:29). But thank God, He who is a consuming fire will be your Saviour if you will trust Him. But you must come God's way. "Neither is there salvation in any other: for there is none other name under heaven given among men, whereby we must be saved" (Ac 4:12, KJV). The blood of Christ is the basis of salvation. Thank God for the blood of Christ!

There's a second thing I'd like to say. The blood of Christ is the basis of our daily cleansing. In 1 John 1:7 we read: "But if we walk in the light, as he is in the light, we have fellowship one with another, and the blood of Jesus his Son cleanseth us from all sin."

May I point out that this book of 1 John has to do with fellowship. You see that from the very outset. Look at verse 3: "That which we have seen and heard declare we unto you also, that ye also may have fellowship with us: yea, and our fellowship is with the Father, and with his Son Jesus Christ." The whole book may be divided in view of fellowship with God. That is what is before us in verse 7. We have fellowship with one another. I take it that that means we have fellowship with other Christians, but I think the primary thrust is that we have fellowship with God. What does verse 3 say? "That ye also may have fellowship with us." That is involved, but notice also, "our fellowship is with the Father, and with his Son Jesus Christ." So verse 7 is dealing with this matter of fellowship with fellow Christians and with God.

Notice that the passage begins like this: "If we walk in the light, as he is in the light, we have fellowship one with another." What does it mean, to walk in the light? Well, it is placed over against what is said in verse 6, walking in darkness. I recognize that, but how do we walk in the light? You say, "Oh, that's too much for me. That's beyond me." Now wait a moment. Let's see what it really says here. It says, "If we walk in the light, as he is in the light, we have fellowship one with another, and the blood of Jesus his Son cleanseth us from all sin." Do you follow this? Are you able to understand this? This business of walking in the light does not mean sinlessness, because if it meant sinlessness you wouldn't need the blood of Christ to cleanse you. But that blood of Christ keeps on cleansing us, restoring us to fellowship, even when we walk in the light—indeed, only when we walk in the light.

Now I want to emphasize a matter here. We all need a good allopathic dose of humility, not the least the one who is speaking to you. So may I remind you, even those of you who know the Lord, even those of you who are walking most closely to the Lord, of something the Lord Jesus said? You find it in Luke 16:15: "And he said unto them [the Pharisees], Ye are they that justify yourselves in the sight of men." I don't know what this does to you, but I know God has excoriated me with this verse because it's so true. "Ye are they that justify yourselves in the sight of men; but God knoweth your hearts." Now here is the principle and here is what I want us to see: "for that which is exalted among men is an abomination in the sight of God." The things for which men will praise you the most are an abomination in the sight of God. I have to admit that even in my most holy moments when my heart is drawn out toward God, when I want the will of God, I am not perfect in myself. I need the blood of Christ. And if I am to have fellowship with the Lord, this is the way I have it, because the blood of Jesus Christ, God's Son, keeps on cleansing from all sin. Thank God for the blood of Christ! It is basic to salvation. It is basic to fellowship with the Lord.

But I'm not through. Quickly let me give you the third item. You'll find it in Revelation 12. There is coming a day of triumph, there is coming a day of glorious victory. "Now is come the salvation, and the power, and the kingdom of our God . . . for the accuser of our brethren is cast down, who accuseth them before our God day and night" (v. 10). This enemy, this accuser, is spoken of in verse 9 as the devil and Satan, and the deceiver of the whole world. He is spoken of as the accuser of the brethren in verse 10. But I want you to see what it says in verse 11: "And they [the brethren] overcame him because of the blood of the Lamb, and because of the word of their testimony; and they loved not their life even unto death."

Actually there are three things there, but I am going to take just the first one: "They overcame him because of the blood of the Lamb." May I suggest to you that the blood of Christ is the basis of victory for the child of God, or reigning in life for the child of God. Listen to the hymn writer:

> He breaks the power of cancelled sin,
>   He sets the prisoner free;
> His blood can make the foulest clean;
>   His blood availed for me.

Thank you, Charles Wesley. Thank you particularly for that first line: "He breaks the power of cancelled sin." Thank God, He cancels it so that you and I do not have to face our sins at the judgment of God.

He cancels sin, but He does something more. He can break the power of that cancelled sin so that I do not have to be the dupe of the devil. I do not have to be the bondslave of the devil. Listen to Toplady:

> Rock of Ages, cleft for me,
> Let me hide myself in Thee;
> Let the water and the blood,
> From Thy riven side which flowed,
> Be of sin the double cure.

What did he mean? Well, let him answer:

> Cleanse me from its guilt and power.

Sin shall not have dominion over you! You know one of the reasons why? The Lord Jesus shed His blood. "They overcame him by the blood of the Lamb."

I have been a pastor, and I have been in administrative posts of

Moody Bible Institute for many, many years. Don't you think, my dear friends, that those years have all passed in tranquility. Don't you think that there have not been times when the devil has gotten his licks in and he in great power has pushed me down into the dust of defeat, for his attacks have been severe—not only against me personally, but against the work of God; and my heart has been broken, and I have shed tears.

I had a mother who loved the Lord. She taught me almost from earliest years, "Son, when the devil comes in like a flood, when the power of the enemy seems irresistible, at that moment, claim the power of the blood of Christ, for He overcame the devil at the cross." And at least in a limited fashion, I can say it is true! I have seen him turn and run before the blood of Christ. They overcame him by the blood of the Lamb.

So I think you see why I love the blood of Christ. It is the basis of salvation. It is the basis of fellowship. It is the basis of victory. There is a hymn which is used at English Keswick again and again. The last stanza runs like this:

> Love's resistless currents sweeping
>   All the regions deep within,
> Thought, and wish, and senses keeping
>   Now and every instant clean;
> Full salvation, full salvation
>   From the guilt and power of sin.

Will you claim that as your blood-bought heritage, your blood-bought right before God? Behold, the Lamb of God, who taketh away the sins of the world!

1971
Distinctives of the Christian Faith

I WANT TO SPEAK on some distinctive elements in the Christian evangel. Let me read several texts which have come to mind in this connection.

> Now therefore fear Jehovah, and serve him in sincerity and in truth; and put away the gods which your fathers served beyond the River, and in Egypt; and serve ye Jehovah. And if it seem evil unto you to serve Jehovah, choose you this day whom ye will serve; whether the gods which your fathers served that were beyond the River, or the gods of the Amorites, in whose land ye dwell: but as for me and my house, we will serve Jehovah (Jos 24:14-15).
>
> There is no God else besides me, a just God and a Saviour; there is none besides me. Look unto me, and be ye saved, all the ends of the earth; for I am God, and there is none else (Is 45:21-22).
>
> For though there be that are called gods, whether in heaven or on earth; as there are gods many, and lords many; yet to us there is one God, the Father, of whom are all things, and we unto him; and one Lord, Jesus Christ, through whom are all things and we through him (1 Co 8:5-6).

The early Christians, those who had blood to shed for their convictions, refused to allow an image of Christ to be placed in the Pantheon, not alone because of the idolatry involved. These soldiers of Christ caught the true significance of Christianity as of another genius than any other faith. The Christian faith to them was not one among equals; it was not even first among equals. It stood alone, unique, preeminent. The conjunctions were never both/and, but always either/or.

There are many evidences of the divine origin of Christianity, and there are many distinctive elements in its evangel. While other faiths may have certain tenets which are also in the Christian evangel, Christianity has many distinctive elements. Think of some. There is the doctrine of the Trinity, the holy Trinity: Father, Son and Holy Spirit—three Persons, one God. This doctrine of the Trinity has its concomitants: the deity of the Son of God and the personality of the Holy Spirit. Here is a Christian distinctive. Second, there is the Christian view of man with its paradox that man is so bad that he cannot prepare himself to come before God, yet he's so valuable that God became incarnate and died to save him. A third distinctive is the fine precision, the exquisite balance that makes grace abound while justice is held inviolate. Fourth, there is the fact that Christianity is the only faith which is bound indissolubly with the person of its Founder, for Christianity is an historic faith. It is rooted in definite acts of history. Fifth, Christianity is the only faith whose Founder is alive, risen from the dead. Sixth, Christianity is the only faith which provides the dynamic which ultimately guarantees the realization of its ethic. Here theory is translated into life, doctrine into deed, creed into character and conduct. From this list, which undoubtedly could be multiplied, I'd like to take two items: (1) Christianity as an historic faith, and (2) Christianity as providing the dynamic for the realization of its ethic.

First, then, Christianity is an historic faith. You may take away the name and the works of the founders of other faiths and it will do little to affect them; the faith is left intact. Outside the telling of the faith's history, the founder may be divorced from its content and message. Not so with Christianity. Take the name of the Lord Jesus Christ from Christianity and what do you have left? Nothing. To use Griffith Thomas's aphorism, "Christianity is Christ." Its convictions are convictions about Him. Its hopes are inspired by Him and He is necessary to their fulfillment. Its ideals are born not only of His teaching but also of His life. Its strength is the strength of His Spirit. Christianity rests upon Him—His perfect deity, His perfect humanity, His sinlessness, His atoning death, His glorious resurrection, His victorious ascension, and His triumphant return. Take Him away, and Christianity evaporates and vanishes from sight.

The facts stated above make Christianity an historic faith. We must be concerned about historicity. Liberalism and neoorthodoxy may dismiss the Bible as history, insisting only on its morals and its so-called truth; but those of us who are orthodox, who are fundamental, cannot do this. By every honest test the foundation stones of the person and work of our Lord stand. If He is not what He claimed to be, if He did not do what He claimed to do and what is claimed for Him as having done, then Christianity is a tissue of falsehood and a fabrication of lies. But the records of the Bible stand; history, archeology, and personal experience corroborate His truth.

A new book is to be made available this week by Moody Press. It is a book containing sixteen messages by Dwight Lyman Moody, edited by Dr. Wilbur M. Smith. Interestingly enough, as I looked at the book I found a sermon entitled "Their Rock Is Not Our Rock." Mr. Moody back in the last century made reference in that sermon to two men whom I had already determined to allude to in this sermon. So it seemed to me I was in apostolic succession. I'm going to refer to these two men now.

It was an uncertain, faltering Lord Littleton who in the eighteenth century studied the record of Paul's conversion and felt that the discrepancies of it and the failure of it to measure up to legal precision would be the undoing of the New Testament history. Lord Littleton studied the record of Paul's conversion, but by every legal test the document proved to be a true record, and he was led to Christ. He wrote an essay entitled "Lord Littleton on the Conversion of Saint Paul." Now this is ancient history; he did this in 1747. The document is still available. In fact, the form that it is in in our library, is spoken of as *Christian Literature: Evidences* and was published in Edinburgh, Scotland, in 1810. (While the essay is longer than normal and would occupy your attention for some length of time, I nevertheless commend it to you.) The fields of history and archeology as well as personal experience, I repeat, corroborate the truth of the Word of God.

The other man was Gilbert West. Let me approach what he had to say on this basis: More than one foe of Christianity has admitted that, if the resurrection of Jesus Christ actually took place, then Christianity must be what it claims to be—a unique, divine, supreme revelation. It should be apparent that any attempt to characterize the resurrection as unessential is really to strike a vital blow at Christianity. The surest road to the dissolution of the Christian faith is to have its advocates repudiate its doctrines and minimize their importance. That the resurrection of the Lord is the pivotal point of attack was understood even by the ancient foes of the faith, as witness the attack of Celsus. On the other hand, this doctrine of the resurrection of Christ has been regarded by believers as the point of tremendous strength.

The infidel jurist, Gilbert West, set out to prove Christianity erroneous by a close study of the records of the resurrection. As a result of that investigation, he became an earnest believer; and from a legal standpoint his work on the Lord's resurrection remains a monumental contribution, even though it was first published in 1747, the same year that Lord Littleton wrote his essay. (You will find this treatise in the same volume mentioned above.)

Christianity is grounded in history. Here is solid fact. Here is substance that can be verified. Here is history. There is no will-o-the-wisp here, no mystical voice, no ectoplasmic visitant. Christianity is based on the acts of God in history. I think this fact should give us comfort and certitude and conviction in our preaching. The Christian faith is not merely a theory finely spun by a genius. It is based on the actual life and death and resurrection and ascension and returning of the Lord Jesus. It is an historic faith and this distinguishes it from other world faiths. I recognize that this is not the age for emphasizing distinctives. This is the age for telling what is common to all faiths. But I would remind you that we have an obligation in trueness to the Lord and to His Word to emphasize the distinctives; and I, without apology, do so.

First, Christianity is an historic faith. Second, Christianity provides the dynamic for its ethic. Some years ago a quotation came to my attention which I want to share with you now.

Perish the thought! Whoever thought Bertrand Russell would be quoted from the pulpit of Moody Bible Institute! Here was an unbeliever; here was a man who stood for things diametrically opposed to the things Moody Bible Institute stands for. But in one moment of weakness during lectures he gave at Columbia University in 1950, Bertrand Russell mused this way:

> The root of the matter is a very simple and old-fashioned thing, a thing so simple I am almost ashamed to mention it, for fear of the derisive smile at which my cynics will greet my words. The thing I mean, please forgive me for mentioning, is love, Christian love, or compassion. If you feel this, you have a motive for existence, a guide in action, a reason for courage, an imperative necessity for intellectual honesty.*

That's an interesting word. When he got down to the root of the matter, when he tried to find that which would bring to pass his ideals, he had to resort to Christian love. Oh, I know this doesn't prove that he was a believer, but I think it was a great admission. I think we have an inkling here, men and women, young men and young woman, of the answer to the realization of the ideals of Christianity. Here is a hint at the dynamic Christian life.

Another man whom you would not expect me to quote speaks to this same theme. Dr. William Ernest Hocking, American philosopher, is coeditor of *Rethinking Missions,* which certainly took its beating from our predecessors at Moody Bible Institute and rightly so. He said this:

> The question, How is love to God or to men possible if as a fact I do not have? would be answered if there were, as the moving spirit of the world, an aggressive lover able and disposed to break in upon my temper of critical egoism and win my response. This would seem to be a necessary, if not a sufficient condition of "salvation."†

Beloved, that's what we believe. A divine lover has broken in upon the stream of human history and has proven His love, for He loved us and gave Himself for us. Out of that ministry of the Son of God, out of that fact of human history, is the very possibility of the dynamic of the Christian ethic. Now, in the few moments I have left, without trying to exhaust the subject, let me suggest to you certain of the dynamics which God has provided so that you and I will enter into the Christian ideal, the Christian ethic.

---

*Bertrand Russell, "Science and Values," in *The Impact of Science on Society,* Matchette Foundation Lectures, no. 3 (New York: Columbia U., 1950), p. 59.
†Wm. E. Hocking, *Human Nature and Its Remaking* (New Haven, Conn.: Yale U., 1918).

May I remind you, first of all, that the very capacity to respond to the teaching of the Holy Spirit in the Word of God depends upon the believer's being a new man in Christ Jesus. When you came to the Saviour, Christian, God imparted life, divine life, to you. And in that rests the very possibility of communication with heaven, for I remind you that the natural man understandeth not the things of the Spirit of God. They are foolishness to him and he cannot know them. Divine revelation is apprehended only by those in whom God has wrought life. This is one of the reasons, pardon me, why some of the world's great leave me absolutely cold when they speak against the Bible and against the God of the Bible. They may be brilliant otherwise. Early in my training in one of the schools I attended there was such a teacher, brilliant in his field of sociology but, when he came to speak about the Bible, utterly foolish. He gave expression to ideas that the text itself could not support.

My friend, you need life. As George Henderson so quaintly put it, "The Bible is unlike every other book in the world in that to understand it you must know its Author." The impartation of life, think of it! I, a mortal here on earth, a sinner by birth, by nature, by choice, have been given the inestimable privilege of being a son of God and of having the life of God, eternal life, in my heart. So if I am to realize the gospel ethic, at least the foundation has been laid and communication is possible between God and myself, between myself and God.

Think again of the language that is used in Scripture to identify what God did when He made you a new creature in Christ Jesus. Look at Ephesians 4:23-24: "Be renewed in the spirit of your mind, and put on the new man, that after God hath been created in righteousness and holiness of truth." The very things God loves, He's given you the capacity to love. The things God hates, He's given you the capacity to hate, for the new man has been created in righteousness and holiness of truth. You have the same idea developed in a little different terminology in Colossians 3:10: "Put on the new man, that is being renewed unto knowledge after the image of him that created him." So first I would answer that the dynamic for Christian living is the impartation of life, divine life. This does not guarantee that we will live as we ought to live, but it does at least set up the possibility. That's what I'm emphasizing at this point.

In the second place, He's given us the Word of God. The Word of God is the enlightener of men, the instrument used of God in regeneration, the revealer of the will and way of God for His children, the disclosure of the prophetic events yet to take place. But it is more, for, listen, it's so simple: when the Word of God is hidden in the heart of God's child, it has power to help the child live a godly life. I need no other text than Psalm 119:11, "Thy word have I hid in mine heart, that I might not sin against thee" (KJV). After all, it is God's Word; it is God's final and full revelation. We do not look for further revelation from God, for it is given to us in the Word of God. If we had no other text than Hebrews 1:1, "God, having of old time spoken unto the fathers in the prophets by divers portions and in divers manners, hath at the end of these days spoken unto us in his Son" that would be enough. The New Testament is the revelation of the Son of God whether it be in the gospels, the book of Acts, the epistles, or the book of the Revelation. All that we need from God for life is revealed to us in that Book. So I assert again, it is God's final and full revelation. I take my stand on the Reformation position that this Book of God is God's full and final Word to men. Nothing compares with it.

It says at the front of the auditorium that God has magnified His Word above all His name (Ps 138:2). Let that sink into your hearts. Do you realize its implications? The great, holy, majestic, glorious, wonderful name of God and God puts His Word above all His glorious name! Don't trifle with that Word. Don't speak disparagingly of that Word. You will be accountable to the God of that Word. Mr. Moody used to say, as it was written on the flyleaf of his Bible, "This book will keep me from sin or sin will keep me from this book." True holiness of life will never result from a casual attitude toward the Bible. You neglect the Bible and you will not know scriptural holiness. If there is in our hearts any aspiration for holiness, if implanted by the Spirit of God there is a deep desire for Christ-likeness, then we can be absolutely sure that the Holy Spirit will lead us to make much of the Word of God. No one who has at his disposal the blessed Book of God and neglects this Book, can be a strong, holy Christian.

Third, the indwelling Lord Himself is provision for us to enter into the Christian ideal; and what shall I say here? I can only give a passing remark in this connection. The Lord Jesus in seven succinct monosyllables encompassed the whole doctrine of our identification with Him when He said in John 14:20: "ye in me, and I in you." I have told the story before; let me tell it again. One of my teachers in early days was speaking to me in his home in central Pennsylvania. As I was about to leave him, I had the temerity to ask him a question—not because I didn't know the answer, but because I wanted to hear it from his lips. I said, "My brother, you have often said you make it the practice of your life upon waking in the morning to first thank God that your body is the temple of the Spirit of God." "Yes, that's right." I said, "Why do you do that?" He replied, "My brother, first of all I want that truth to live. I want it to be vital and vibrant. I want it to be known and realized in my life every day that my body is a temple of the Spirit of God." "Yes," I said, "and what else?" He said so simply and yet so helpfully, "And second, it makes a difference in the way I live."

Look, if the Lord Jesus is living in your body—and the Bible says He is—it seems to me that, entirely apart from all the divine power and all the authority that is His to order His will, apart from the infusion of His power to the surrendering soul, it is enough of a tremendous incentive for holy living just to realize that He who is God of God, and Light of light, and very God of very God, is living in me. Oh, what a thought! Oh, what a tremendous thought to make me live as I ought to live.

The fourth dynamic, and I must say this briefly, is the return of Christ. I have in mind not only the fact that He may come at any time and I ought to live now in the light of His coming. That's important, that has its place; but that's not the emphasis I have on my mind and heart right now. It is this, rather, that 1 John 3:2 says: "When he shall appear, we shall be like him" (KJV).

Look, if Christianity is to be worthy of its name, you and I sooner or later, someplace or other, have to arrive at perfection, the likeness of Christ. In the meanwhile, may we increase more and more and advance from glory to glory. God has arranged that His ethic will be fully fashioned, and it is part of that which makes for the veracity and the credibility and the thoroughness of Christianity.

Our citizenship is in heaven from whence we look for the Saviour, who shall fashion anew the body of our humiliation and conform us to the body of His glory. He is coming, and in that the ethic of the Bible will be fully realized.

So I suggest to you not to try to find points of similarity, but to major on the differences, the distinctives. May we never forget these two: Christianity is an historic faith, rooted and grounded in acts of God in history; and Christianity provides the dynamic for the realization of its ethic, now and ultimately.